WITHDRAWN

ANYWHERE OUT OF THE WORLD

Also by Nicholas Delbanco

ANYWHERE
OUT OF THE WORLD

Essays on Travel, Writing, Death

Nicholas Delbanco

COLUMBIA UNIVERSITY PRESS

NEW YORK

Columbia University Press

Publishers Since 1893

New York   Chichester, West Sussex

Copyright © 2005 Nicholas Delbanco

Library of Congress Cataloging-in-Publication Data

Delbanco, Nicholas.

Anywhere out of the world : essays on travel, writing, death / Nicholas Delbanco.

p. cm.

ISBN 0–231–13384–7 (acid-free paper)

1. Delbanco, Nicholas. 2. Authors, American—20th century—Biography. 3. Delbanco,
Nicholas—Friends and associates. 4. Voyages and travels. 5. Authorship. I. Title.

PS3554.E442Z64   2005

809—dc22

2004050212

∞

Columbia University Press books are printed on permanent and durable acid-free paper.

Printed in the United States of America

c 10 9 8 7 6 5 4 3 2 1

For
Francesca and Andrea
Dearest of daughters, both

Contents

Acknowledgments

"In Praise of Imitation" appeared in *Harper's* Magazine, Vol. 305, No. 1826, July 2002, pp. 57–63. "Anywhere Out of the World" appeared in *Harper's* Magazine, September, 2004, pp. 91–96.

"The Dead" includes extracts from my introduction to *Stillness and Shadows*, two posthumously published novels by John Gardner (New York: Knopf, 1986); from my *Running in Place: Scenes from the South of France* (New York: Atlantic Monthly Press, 1989) and from my contribution to *What These Ithakas Mean: Readings in Cavafy* (Athens: Hellenic Literary and Historical Archive, 2002).

"An Old Man Mad About Writing" appeared in "History and Representation in Ford Madox Ford's Writings," ed. Max Saunders, *International Ford Madox Ford Quarterly*, vol. 3 (Amsterdam and New York: Rodopi, 2004), 219–232.

"Letter from Namibia' appeared in *Salmagundi*, Winter–Spring 2004, Nos. 141–142, pp. 170–198.

"On *Daniel Martin*" appeared in *Brick*, Fall 2001, number 68, pp. 92–100.

A very different version of "Strange Type" first appeared in *Five Points*, Vol. 14, No. 3, Summer 2000, pages 19–34.

ANYWHERE OUT OF THE WORLD

In Praise of Imitation

Our president is famously ill at ease with English. The jokes proliferate; the verbal stumblebummings (from a Yalie yet! A millionaire!) endear him to those who believe him endearing and outrage those who don't. In the country of the blind, the one-eyed man is chief executive, and that quick study who before him occupied the White House has been displaced in an eye blink, a wink. This current spate of malapropisms (state of malatropism? Malappropriatism?) seems likely to continue, and to stay part of the picture; Mr. Bush will not, I mean, reveal a sudden interest in Tolstoi or a schoolboy's devotion to Proust. For better or for worse, such "Aw-shucks" analphabetic ignorance is part of his leadership profile and accruing lore.

What seems strange in this regard is the emphasis on education, the presidential insistence that a school be held accountable for the test scores of its students, the platform plank that children—as opposed to elected officials—must improve their reading skills. We worry as a nation about declining SAT results and what achievements they measure; we propose their abolition or vouch for the value of vouchers or celebrate home schools instead. It's as though the tone-deaf took the podium in concert halls or the color-blind

selected what hangs in a museum. This is one of the para-
doxes intrinsic to democracy: the less you know about a case,
the less you need to recuse yourself from serving as a judge.
It's the mode of operation that obtains during jury selection:
we pick only those twelve who know nothing about it to settle the lawsuit at hand. . . .

And therefore I wish to propose—not tongue-in-cheek
but earnestly—a return to ancient ways. There was a time
when those who led were those we wished to follow, and
study was a course of emulation: *Repeat, class, after me*. Such
a system is tradition-steeped but now may seem original; at
any rate, it's how our parents' parents—in ways we've forgotten—were taught.

These lines urge imitation, and in the spirit of praise. The
habit begins in the cradle; we copy what we watch. We learn
from those who learned before to walk and dress and brush
our teeth and play tennis or the violin; it's how we come to
spell and drive and swim. It's the way we first acquire language and, later, languages. *What does the cow say? Moo, moo!*
That golden codger lifting arms and clapping hands while a
grandchild does the same is teaching by repeated gesture:
How big is baby? So-o-o big! From the way to eat an artichoke
or lobster, the way to fashion a "hospital corner" or bow tie,
from birth to death and *alpha* to *omega*, the elders of the tribe
instruct us by example. And if what we study is writing, it's
surely how we learn to write; all writers read all the time.

Often this process of replication is unconscious or only
partly conscious. We hear a line and repeat it; we memorize
the words of a joke or ceremony or play. The human race re-
produces itself, as do snow leopards and snow peas; the
genome project undertakes to map this landscape of transmission: how and why. What imitation helps us map is how
the artist works and why, and knowledge of that process will
shape informed response.

As a writer and teacher of writing, I get textbooks in the
mail with disconcerting frequency. They bulk large every

term. Each year some ballyhooed new version of what arrived last year arrives, and each year I unwrap it and groan.
Like most of my colleagues, I imagine, I put such volumes in
the hall or on the English department's "free" bookshelf and
hope some passing someone may discover something useful
and haul the pages away. There's nothing quite so sad or
reeking of futility as the used textbooks section of a used
bookstore; the editions (New and Revised! New and Updat-
ed!! New and Expanded!!!) grow quickly old.

Yet few if any of those books propose a methodology familiar in most other disciplines: standard practice where
standards obtain. No introductory text in math or Spanish
would suggest that the student should go it alone; rather,
their chapters are structured to permit sequential entry into a
language others have practiced, and practice is the norm. In
the Palmer method (of learning handwriting) and the Suzu-
ki method (of learning to play a musical instrument) such a
system of "mimicry" continues. Rote learning—the recital
of verb forms or multiplication tables in class—has been dis-
credited as a teaching technique, but it did have its points.

For imitation is deep-rooted as a mode of cultural transmission; we tell our old stories again and again. The bard-in-
training had to memorize long histories verbatim, saying or
singing what others had sung. In the oral-formulaic tradition, indeed, the system *required* retentiveness; you listened
to your master's tale until you could recite, say, *The Wanderer* or *Beowulf* for the next generation. There are some
places in the world where such a tradition still operates, but
in the West we've largely lost it; it's at best a vestigial skill.
Since the invention of moveable type and ever-increasing
access to books, there's been less need for oral recitation and
trained aural memory. A "photographic" memory is more
common now than a "phonographic" one, and with the current shift in publishing from page to screen, that displacement will no doubt continue.

As recently as Shakespeare's time, however, the plays
were remembered, not written down; what we have of
Romeo and Juliet and *Antony and Cleopatra* is largely what

the playwright's colleagues *heard*. Memorization, copying, recitation in unison, transcribing whole passages verbatim: all these systems of instruction were established centuries ago. It should therefore be acknowledged that what I'm proposing may seem original—innovative in the class-room, experimental in its emphases—but it's an ancient technique. It's a question not of inventing the wheel but of watching it turn on a time-honored track. Such practice re-wards the apprentice as well as those far advanced in the trade; we all are members—readers and writers, students and teachers—of a single guild.

Sweeping assertions, brave claims. They need some spelling out.

In *Webster's New Collegiate Dictionary*, "imitation" is de-fined as follows:

> 1. An imitating; a copying. 2. That which is made or produced as a copy; an artificial likeness. 3. Properly, a literary work de-signed to reproduce the style or manner of another author. 4. *Biol.* Mimicry. 5. *Music.* The repetition in a voice part of the melodic theme; phrase or motive previously found in another part. Imitation is *strict* when the original theme or phrase and its repeated form are identical in intervals and note values, *free* when the repetition has some modification.[1]

As the fourth of these brief definitions suggests, the act of mimicry is well established in nature. The coat of mountain goats and skin tint of chameleons blend in with the rock face and leaf. A mockingbird borrows its song. *All* life, it can be argued, depends on imitation; from the pattern of cells in mitosis to the pattern of fish shoals and swallows in flight there's repetition entailed. The usage that compels me here, however, is less the biological sense of mimicry than "imita-tion"'s second dictionary meaning of "a copy; an artificial likeness." Though the salmon and the polar bear may inher-it via instinct their system of behavior, those who "reproduce the style or manner of another author" must study what they do.

In music and the visual arts, "free" repetition is common; both eye and ear acknowledge variations on a theme. We salute the work of others in a musical arrangement or a composition structured as a predecessor painted it; this process of quotation is familiar. In museums everywhere there's someone hunched over a sketch pad or easel, copying what's framed and on the wall. The techniques of mimicry—and its silent partner, mime—prove crucial to the actor's craft, taking center stage. To imitate another's gait or accent is to refine interpretation: we borrow a character's limp or lisp so as to make that character our own.

In most forms of performance, indeed, we take such skills for granted—and personal expressiveness may even be a mistake. The members of a dance troupe must follow their choreographer's lead, moving in trained unison, and woe betide that member of the string section of an orchestra who chooses an exotic bowing. Such sedulous aping is not the exception but rule. To be singled out while joining in a chorus is to risk correction; when you march, you should do so in step.

Overheard at the Fifth Avenue parade: "Look, Rachel, my Johnny's the only one in step!"

I'm not suggesting that protective coloration need be drab, or that not to be noticed is best. But for many centuries and in many different cultural contexts, the standard of imitation and close reproduction held sway. It was how to learn a trade. An apprentice in a studio would have mixed paint or cleaned the varnish rags and swept wood shavings from the floor for what must have felt like forever, only slowly and under supervision might the young artisan approach the canvas or the cabinet itself. Large compositions by Old Masters have soldiers and horses and meadows and clouds roughed in by their assistants; the picture is "authentic" nevertheless. The wooden stringed-instrument maker J. B. Vuillaume took his patterns unabashedly from his much-admired predecessor Stradivari. This is not forgery so much as emulation, a willing admission that others have gone that way before. . . .

Nor is mimicry confined to craftsmanship and the creative or performing arts. In middle age, we find ourselves repeating what our parents said; as candidates for political office, we recite slogans time after time while pounding the pavement for votes. At the ticket counter or in the fast-food take-out line, the dictates of efficiency make a virtue out of sameness; the entire profit system of the industrial age—mass production and conveyor belts—is based on uniformity. Component parts must be interchangeable and therefore identical in manufactured products; it's wasteful to start every module from scratch or guess at the size of a gear. To a greater or lesser degree, it would seem, *all* ritual observance partakes of repetition. Religion thrives on it, as do medicine and soldiering and law.

So why should we exempt the writer's learning process from, as *Webster's* puts it, "an imitating, a copying"? We've grown so committed as a culture to the ideal of originality that the artist who admits to working in the manner of another artist will likely stand accused of being second-rate. But to imitate is not to be derivative; it's simply to admit we derive from what was accomplished by others. The botanical meaning of "derivation," indeed, has to do with grafting and putting forth new shoots. In our pursuit of self-expression, we've forgotten the old adage: "There is no new thing under the sun."

Another famous phrase puts the case precisely: "Imitation is the sincerest form of flattery." If asked, nine readers out of ten would recite the line as I've transcribed it. But they would be wrong. The actual quotation, according to Bartlett—who got it right—comes from a book of aphorisms called *The Lacon*, by George Caleb Colton (1780–1832). The line he wrote and none of us remember is "Imitation is the sincerest of flattery."[2] Colton himself makes no mention of form.

Yet by the alchemy of a collective consciousness, "form" enters in nevertheless. The sentence seems to need it, and not merely for the sake of the additional syllable. Always implicit in the idea of copying, "form" here becomes explicit. So this is an example of *Webster's* fifth definition of "free" or inexact imitation, where "the repetition has some modification." And although its author has been long forgotten, the line he didn't write is widely quoted now.

"Sincerity" and "imitation" when conjoined in the writing of fiction are, on the face of it, strange bedfellows; as writers we weave fantasies and hope to be believed. We make up situations and invent characters whole cloth in order to persuade the reader of our imagined truth. We create a scene in dialogue, suggesting that it's audible and in silence overheard. If art is mimesis—a Greek word meaning imitation of reality—then it's done with smoke and mirrors and twenty-six letters in an agreed-on sequence; we pretend that there's a world within the word. The alphabet is merely a convention, after all, and so are the rules of grammar and spacing; what law of nature has ordained that "the" not be spelled "eht"? Or, come to that, XXY?

Such matters of convention—of recognized shared pretense—lie at the root of modernism, of postmodernism when acknowledged; the artist grows self-conscious while wielding pen or brush. The very notion of "a mirror held to nature" has been modified, and the artificial aspect of the act of copying is stressed. To be "sincere" or "more sincere" or "sincerest" is still to lie for a living, and even the confessional author has to shape his or her tale. So there's an appropriate irony in the widespread addition of "form" to Colton's phrase: it's a quasi-quotation, half-truth.

"Antonello da Massina was serving as an apprentice in his master's studio. The commission was nearly complete, the master engaged on his self-portrait in the lower right-hand corner, behind the donor's image—a kind of signature. Then he was bitten by a disease-bearing mosquito and fell ill. From his sickbed he issued the order that the project be completed; from what looked as if it might prove his death-bed, he rose to examine the work. At first sight of the commission he pronounced himself well pleased. Looking more closely, however, at what was no longer a self-portrait in progress but a completed portrait he leaned forward to inspect a black speck on the neck.

"'What's this?' he inquired of Antonello. 'What is this?'

"'Master,' said his student, deferential, 'that's the mosquito that so nearly killed you.'

"The painter doffed his cap. 'Antonello,' he announced, 'you're the master now.'"[3]

I first heard this story from an elderly Italian thirty years ago; I have told it often since. As with any anecdote whose telling is habitual, the lines and dialogue and intonation, the gestures and the pauses have grown fixed. Too, I place it in quotation marks because I used it previously in a lecture on the nature of apprenticeship, then printed it in an essay called "Judgment" in 1991 and, thereafter, in a book. I cite/recite myself. It would have been simple enough, no doubt, to refashion the language a little and change the mosquito to a tse-tse fly and pretend that the anecdote's new. The fear of repetition is, for this writer, real.

But what's the point of attempting now to alter or better what was sufficient before? As a description of achievement, of artistic independence earned, this seems to me as useful and instructive today as when I first heard it from a long-dead acquaintance over drinks. By now the story's mine, not his, and who knows how or from whom he in his turn appropriated it? Perhaps it may, some seasons hence, be told by someone who reads it here and responds as I did then. . . .

It might be worth admitting, however, that I have no idea if the story's true or false, if Antonello finished the portrait or not and if his master doffed his cap. I neither consulted a sourcebook nor looked for the painting itself. This is cultural transmission of the casual, not to say slapdash, sort; it makes a supportive second-in-command out of what could otherwise have seemed a greedy apprentice, and a self-effacing gentleman out of what might well have been an outraged boss. The twice-told tale gains currency, and if sufficiently dramatic will color collective opinion (Richard III is a villain, Henry V a hero); the routinely repeated invention, over time, overshadows flat fact.

George Colton might perhaps have hoped that all of us would know his name, but the dead don't care. These last four words, if quoted—"The dead don't care"—should properly be assigned to the undertaker-poet Thomas Lynch, who uses them repeatedly and to excellent effect in his recent essays on mortality. But Lynch himself, I'd hazard, would welcome general usage and not ownership of that phrase; a major form of literary achievement is to enter into common parlance unannounced. "Catch-22," for example, may well outlast the book it titles as it has outlived its author, Joseph Heller—and all of us salt-pepper discourse with phrases we can't locate in terms of their actual source. There's nothing wrong with this; rather, 'tis a consummation devoutly to be wished (*Hamlet* 3.1.71–72).

The bulk of our literature's triumphs have been collective, or anonymous; who can identify the authors of the Bible or the Ramayana? More to the point, who cares? What we know of Homer and Lady Murasaki is, in effect, their texts. This is not to say that their work fails to display personality—the reverse is more nearly true—but rather that the cult of personality should fade. The impulse toward individual expression is a recent and a possibly aberrant one in art; it has nothing to do with the labor—or the creative excitement—of studying writing as such.

So Peter De Vries can add a comma to the opening line of a novel: "Call me, Ishmael," and the inexact quotation is an act of wit. Or Jorge Luis Borges can assert that "Pierre Menard, Author of the Quixote," writes a text no whit inferior to the great original—indeed, more wholly achieved because *conscious* of its antecedent, word for word. John Barth, extolling "The Literature of Exhaustion" in 1967, says, "I myself have always aspired to write Burton's version of *The*

1001 Nights, complete with appendices and the like, in ten volumes, and for intellectual purposes I needn't even write it. What evenings we might spend discussing Saarinen's Parthenon, D. H. Lawrence's *Wuthering Heights,* or the Johnson Administration by Robert Rauschenberg!"[4]

At this forward-facing moment and start of the millennium, it seems we've acquired the Janus-faced habit of also looking back. (Janus is the two-faced Roman god who gave his name to January; poised at the turning of the year, he sees both ways at once.) Michael Cunningham's prize-winning book, *The Hours,* is an extended act of imitation; he enters the world both of a modern-day Clarissa Dalloway and of her creator, Virginia Woolf. The film *Shakespeare in Love* is highly allusive, a good-humored tip of the cap to the language of Elizabethan England; its jokes require knowledge of the plays and playwright it spoofs. Patrick O'Brian's Aubrey and Maturin novels constitute an uninterrupted foray into the imaginative discourse of a world at war 200 years ago, and large swatches of the story pay homage to Jane Austen or borrow from naval accounts. And these are just the iceberg's tip; present examples abound.

This year there'll be another "Faux Faulkner" contest in Oxford, Mississippi, and there are more Hemingway lookalike and write-alike contests than one can shake a fishing rod or a rifle at. There's the "Bulwer-Lytton" contest, in which we're invited to write as badly as possible—to bottom, as it were, his famous opening phrase, "It was a dark and stormy night." One could even argue that the current fad of karaoke and lip-synching is based on a similar premise; the practice requires split-second coordination and, where silent, mimicry. Think of the tasks of translation or dubbing: the translator fails when he or she places a personal stamp on the text at hand; the dubber fails as soon as you notice how good a job's being done.

Imitation is, as well, a time-honored practice in verse. Robert Lowell used precisely that word to describe his own effort of translation from languages he read only a little and sometimes not at all. His book *Imitations* (1962) is a series of original poems inspired by and freely rendering the work of other poets. We call a sonnet "Petrarchan" or "Shakespeare-an" in honor of those who popularized the particular rhyme scheme and stanzaic pattern; we write in the "Miltonic" or "Spenserian" or "Eliotic" mode. The poet William Butler Yeats called apprenticeship a "singing school," and much of his own verse deploys traditional forms. Emily Dickinson and Walt Whitman—two widely admired "originals" of the nineteenth century—have influenced modern practitioners in direct lines of descent. Although self-evident, the point is worth repeating: variations on a theme are commonplace, not rare. Those artists who borrow or adapt a form—*all* artists, in effect—engage in imitation all the time.

In this regard, at least, the early authors had it easier, had fewer doubts. They would have found nothing shameful in prescribed subjects or in avoiding the first-person pronoun. Since the story was a constant one (how Troy was burned, how Rome was built), the apprentice could focus on style. Those writers we admire have a habit of seeing, of *saying* their world, and when we raise eyes from the page we're likely to see as they saw. A copyist must pay the kind of close attention to the model that a counterfeiter does, and though the results may not be original they are, when successful, real proof of technique.

Here's a description, by the late great poet and scholar, A. K. Ramanujan, of the process by which Indian musicians acquire mastery:

> They want the influence. They have all apprenticed them-selves to the master. This is the way traditional Indian mu-sicians will learn. They will sit behind the singer and sing along with him, just droning. Then, gradually, the master will ask the disciple to join his voice to his. He will do it for several years. At the end of it the master is gone, and the dis-ciple is left to sing the song. It is through imitation that you learn. It is through following in the master's line. This was

true of the poets and every other artist. . . . The poet said, "I will show one more thing that the tradition can do."[5]

What George Colton referred to, it should be clear, was neither insincerity nor flattery's forked tongue. There are several forms of flattery in which the tongue is lodged in cheek or the courtier does not mean the praise brought forth in court. But the "sincerest" admits of no such irony or hypocritical double-dealing and must be taken at face value. Colton meant the desire to emulate, and we emulate what we admire.

If "Imitation is the sincerest of flattery," it's because those who copy it wish to be part of the fashion; those who model themselves on others—wearing what the models wear, speaking and moving in preapproved style—do so in the hope that they in turn will be admired. Most of those who copy are respectful of the text (or painting, or hairdo, or way of walking down a street) and try to follow along. Think of that game children play: Simon Says. The whole point is responsiveness, or learning how to follow the leader; when you fail at mimicry, you lose.

This need not, however, be always the case. There's a variety of humor in which the critic or the comic is making fun of what he or she impersonates; consider those comedians who take out after movie stars or politicians, and it's obvious that imitation need not always be sincere. Parody and caricature rely on just such exaggeration. Take a signature component part—a nose, an accent, a way of wearing suits or skirts—and blow it up out of proportion: the part represents the whole. One sure way to get a laugh—or irritate the model, in another game most children play—is simply to repeat. *One sure way to get a laugh—or irritate the model, in another game most children play—is simply to repeat. One sure way to get a laugh*—until we cry, "Enough!"

And this perhaps explains some negative connotations of the word "imitation" itself. The American ideals of "rugged individuality" and "independence" stand in opposition to what we're told we have become, a nation of "con*form*ists."

Often we compare an imitation unfavorably to the original; often we call it counterfeit or mass-produced or fraudulent. In the worst-case academic scenario—unacknowledged quotation—we call it "plagiarism"; in the business scenario it's "copyright infringement" or "intellectual property theft." A "copycat'" is booed, not cheered. A "camp follower" cannot by definition be the leader of the pack. "Herd instinct" will lead us astray. So imitation may be seen as stealing or second-rank invention or, at the least, uninspired; it's a pejorative term.

But those legions who impersonate Elvis do so almost as an act of worship; the majority of those who copy do so in the spirit of praise. They mean to compliment, not insult the model reproduced. When mimicry's sincere, it does connote respect; Colton meant what he wrote, and he's right.

All writers are promiscuous; we fall in love repeatedly—desiring *this* one's knowledge of the world, *that* one's way with character, *this* one's storytelling skill, *that* one's gift of gab. Infatuation of this particular variety requires just an armchair and a reading lamp. In the context of the library, we find ourselves attracted to and study with practitioners we never get to meet. So what passes for originality—a voice we can identify and an inflection recognize—is likely to come from a chorus of the young writer's influential because admired predecessors: borrowings too numerous to name.

In the contemporary classroom, however, the text is all too often relegated to the sideline—as a springboard for discussion, an occasion for debate, a soapbox, or a whipping boy. Too rarely does the student perform what used to be called close analysis or pay sustained attention to the author's language as such. Sincere imitation takes time. You cannot copy what you glance at nor remember what you speed-read nor repeat what you half heard; the reason one writer chooses semicolons, or another elects an apposite comma, or a third prefers the absence of standard punctuation marks has a great deal to do with the worldview expressed, and a compound

sentence will represent a different way of looking at the link-
ages of things—the way the past impinges on the present as
does the present the future in an unbroken line of descent or
argument if represented with a dash—than does a simple or
short. Or a sentence that isn't one, such as this and the suc-
ceeding one word. Sentence.

That writing *is* a craft as well as art is something all accomplished authors take to be self-evident. Every professor
professes it; every student studies it. Practice makes, if not
perfect, a better practitioner; if we swing a baseball bat or
golf club twenty thousand times in order to improve our
game, why not hone the skills of composition too? Such freedom within limits is the root and force of syntax, for each of
us must understand the rules we choose to break.

And this is one of the risks that attaches to early success.
America is cruel-kind to its emerging talent, subjecting it to
overpraise and inflated claims of *authenticity, originality, innovation, genius.* . . . While still apprenticed to a trade, we
may be given walking papers and hailed as a contemporary
master or mistress thereof. As Cyril Connolly mordantly
observed in *Enemies of Promise*, "Young writers, if they are
to mature, require a period of between three and seven years
in which to live down their promise."[6] And, again, "The
best that can happen for a writer is to be taken up very late
or very early, when either old enough to take its measure,
or so young that when dropped by society he has all life before him."[7]

It's important, therefore, that we teach not what to write
but how to write it, since a great weight can be lifted from the
young artist's shoulders if subject matter is predetermined,
not something to invent. It's simply good and common
sense, it's uncommonly good simple sense, and this rhetorical device (where the terms of a phrase are reversed) is called
a *chiasmus*. Note also please the repetitive arrangement of the
eight words of the antepenultimate paragraph's brief second
sentence ("Every professor professes . . ."). The form of *this*
paragraph's previous sentence ("Note also please . . .") is an
imperative; the writer proposes and does not ask (*interroga-*

tive) or describe (*declarative*) what the reader needs to note. The words "need" and "note" are linked at birth, or *cognate* terms; the latter is the German equivalent of the English former. And so on and so forth.

Imitation, I mean, is everywhere—copying, mimicry, echo—and everywhere can serve a purpose in "that which is made or produced."

Back, therefore, to the basics. Imitation is the route—not perhaps the only route, but a well-traveled one—to originality. Let's declare a moratorium on self-expression, self-discovery, self-help: all those inward-facing projects that fail to acknowledge the outward and Janus-faced aspect of prose. Originality is rare indeed, not subject to instruction, and the learning curve of each apprentice describes an upward arc. To copy *Moby-Dick* or "Lycidas" verbatim is to come nearer to great artistry than we can get on our own. And even if there be a young Melville or Milton among us, that writer's self-expression, self-discovery, etc. will be aided by close study of a predecessor's work.

For there's keen-edged discomfiture in starting out again. What we took for granted is no longer ours to take. It's rather like learning to walk or talk via a rehabilitation program and by conscious application after the body—as a result of some disease or trauma—has lost its motor skills. This is, I think, one reason the apprentice (the first-year college student, say) finds English composition such a daunting task. Old habits have to be relearned and old assumptions revised. Consider how we speak or breathe, the intricate nerve ends and musculature entailed, and consider what it would entail to instruct oneself to breathe and speak; so too with the language as such.

Lately I've been teaching with this theory of practice in mind. At both the undergraduate and the graduate levels— with authors such as Faulkner, Hemingway, Joyce, and Woolf as models—I've been asking my students to imitate greatness, to copy (in some cases literally) their separate ways of using the dash, the parenthesis, the ellipsis. . . . It works. It works wonders wonderfully well. It works to demonstrate the way the first of these three sentences works better than the second, why alliterative excess fails, and why this third of our brief triad is in and of itself redundant.

My opening assertion was: *Our president is famously ill at ease with English. The jokes proliferate; the verbal stumblebummings (from a Yalie yet! A millionaire!) endear him to those who believe him endearing and outrage those who don't. In the country of the blind, the one-eyed man is chief executive, and that quick study who before him occupied the White House has been displaced in an eye blink, a wink.* In every act of reading there's an agreement, however unspoken, that we're rehearsing a previous phrase; the very act of printing "copies" consists of repetition. The reader who does not refer to the previous page but can repeat and continue these lines is ready to continue with that reader's own.

The Dead

A student in this century cannot, I think, encounter those two words—"the dead"—without recalling the short story by James Joyce. He owns that title now. In its great last paragraph, the "snow was general all over Ireland," falling equally upon the living and the dead. That those who die remain alive to those who quicken while recalling them seems a near-commonplace of literature as well as life; we stand at the window with Gabriel Conroy and also watch and wait.

But the term itself, "commonplace," need not be a pejorative; it's what we have in common, where we meet. On the collective of the village green or beyond a house party in Dublin, the snow falls for Joyce's protagonist as it did once, in Paris, for François Villon. Yesteryear's snows may have melted, but *les neiges d'antan sont partout.* . . .

The fictive Conroy is imagined, the poet Villon a historical presence, but in our culture's ledger they belong to the same page. Snow angels, snow queens, snow maidens thawing: all these are emblems of winter cajoled into life by warm spring. Those woolly mammoths pinioned in a glacier, those early men preserved down to their boots and tunics by the crevasse containing them: the chill cadavers kept on ice retain their power, motionless, to move. When Ted Williams's children tried to freeze his DNA, they were mounting a campaign against, if not entropy, rot. Snow falls without distinction on the quick and the invented and the dead.

"To everything there is a season," avers Ecclesiastes, and the seasons turn. *What comes around goes around*, and so on and on in predictable tropes: our parents' parents forged a path; we follow where they lead. Science has, of course, provided us with breakthrough knowledge and in some cases with authentically new instances—genetic modification, say, or newly manufactured compounds—of what *can* be known. But the work of the writer, more often than not, has been to tell us yet again what our elders *knew*. If there be such a thing as tradition—a retentive passing on of standards—then that double-edged word "generation" is a crucial component thereof. To the child, perhaps, immortality seems plausible; the young don't think themselves at risk. The middle-aged and senior citizens do what they can to deny it, but death begins with our first breath and draws nearer with the next.

Here's a statistical certainty: all who are born will die. It isn't a question of whether but when, and one of the tasks of the artist is to record how and where. So let me celebrate the dead (a pair of them, at any rate) by remembering, while yet I can, how vivid they were to me once.

The cover illustration of John Gardner's collection of short stories, *The Art of Living*, shows a motorcyclist racing at the reader, straight on. His jacket is black leather, as was John's, and his expression is grim. It is as though he drives *In the Suicide Mountains*—another of that author's titles—prepared to take the leap described on the final page of *Grendel*; there are fierce night rides throughout his work, and creatures everywhere at risk.

John Champlain Gardner Jr. died of injuries sustained in a motorcycle accident on Tuesday, September 14, 1982. The afternoon was balmy, bright; the roads were dry. He was an experienced driver, a few miles from home; he swerved—to avoid another vehicle, perhaps?—and fell. John was forever trying to explain himself, but death is inexplicable; the coroner's report describes result, not cause. It is clear he was trying to make it, fighting to survive. We never will know what he saw while he fell, or felt when the handlebar dealt him its mortal gut punch. He maintained, repeatedly, he had no fear of death; he wanted the rider of *The Art of Living* to appear playful, not fierce. On September 16, two days after the accident, my wife and I received a letter from him full of future plans. He was to marry a third time on what became his funeral weekend; he was immersed in a translation of *Gilgamesh*—"Fine pome!"; he sounded, as always, vividly alive.

John seemed somehow to have been born with a quicker ratio to the passage of time than the rest of us. He worked in a headlong, hurtling rush—at times, twenty hours a day. Each new home for him, I think, was absolutely home; each new set of friends was old and dear and gifted; his moderation was our excess and his excess brooked no containment. It was not so much a forced march and furious pace, as if he knew he might die young and wanted to waste or miss nothing. Rather, it was as if he decided that central matters demanded all his patient seriousness. He had no attention left to squander on sleep or table manners or the IRS. . . .

Others knew him longer and more intimately. I offer this account of friendship in the knowledge it was representative; many share in the loss. We met on Tuesday, April 16, 1974. I was teaching at Bennington College, in Bennington, Vermont, and he was on a reading tour; he and his wife, Joan, arrived for dinner at our house.

My first impression of Gardner remains: a rotund, pipe-smoking man, with a high-pitched voice and rapid rate of utterance, pontificating splendidly and as if by rote. His eyes were red-rimmed, his white hair lank; he made his entry two hours late. It was not his fault, in fact; it was Albany Airport's, and the fog's. But somehow, in the ensuing years, there would always be some such disruption: a car would fail to start or end up in a ditch, a snowstorm would come out of nowhere, a wallet would be misplaced. Joan Gardner wore expensive clothing and fistfuls of jewelry; the novelist wore blue jeans and a cracked black leather vest. He emptied a quart of vodka before he sat to eat.

I saw him often in such situations later; they are hard to avoid. Fame brings a constant, admiring assault, a request from civil strangers to be brilliant or outrageous or at least informed. Its continual wear forces one to substitute a mask for face; sooner or later, they fuse. This is doubly a danger for the writer, since privacy is the *sine qua non* of his work and he has had no training in the actor's life.

By midnight I had dropped my guard; by two o'clock he had too. Elena, my wife, went to bed; Joan stayed at the table and drank. Since I had to teach next morning, I tried to call a halt; I had to prepare for my class. Nonsense, said John, we'd have another bottle and he'd help me through the morning session—what was it on, by the way? "Virginia Woolf," I said, and construed his nodding to mean knowledge of her work. So we talked till four or five and met again at ten o'clock; I weaved my way to class.

In the event, I did most of the teaching. Perhaps I knew more about Virginia Woolf; certainly I felt more responsible to the students than did their visitor. I lectured with a panicky inventiveness, stopping only for questions or breath. The session went well, I knew that. But Gardner assured me, with what I later came to recognize as characteristic hyperbole, that it was the best talk he'd ever attended—at least, on any author after Malory. He knew something more than I did, maybe, about Apollonius of Rhodes. . . . I was gratified, of course, and all the more so when his wife said he repeated the praise to her later; we had become "fast friends." The next night, after his reading, I asked if he wanted a job.

I was in the position to hire him but did not believe he'd accept. It was more an offhand courtesy, a variety of "If you'd ever care to come back through. . . ." To my surprise, he said yes. He was tired of his present appointment, possibly; his family hoped to move east. At the end of *Stillness*— a posthumously published autobiographical novel—he records the accidental-seeming sequence that brought him to Vermont. We were in his motel room; he was changing shirts. This completes my introductory image: a white-fleshed, big-bellied man with his pants legs rolled up, his pipe smoking on the coverlet, and papers all over the bed. Students clustered at the motel entrance, waiting to whisk him away. The last thing that he handed me was a drawing of himself as gnome, peeping out from behind bushes, with the block-letter legend, "Should Nicholas require John Gardner, he can be reached at . . ." his number and address in Illinois. I did require him, and he could be reached.

For three years thereafter, we saw each other continually. His presence was a gift. He ballyhooed my work in public and berated it in private. Day in, week out, we wrangled over prose. There was nothing polite or distanced about his sense of colleagueship; if he hated a line he said so, and if he hated a character he said so all the more loudly. At this remove it's hard to remember what we discussed at such length: profluence, *energeia*, walnut trees. I spent three days hunting through graveyards and telephone books in order to prove that Sherbrooke with an *e*—the surname of a character in the novel I was writing—would be more likely than Sherbrook without. He came up with a whiskey bottle spelled Sherbrook; I pointed to a Sherbrooke township south of Montreal. We co-taught classes and founded a summer writing workshop together. Out of many memories, I will here cite two.

October Light was accorded the National Book Critics Circle Award for fiction in 1976. The presentation ceremony took place in New York, and John's publishers made it an occasion. They hosted a supper party afterward, and a suite was reserved in Gardner's name at the Algonquin Hotel. He asked Elena and me to be his companions that night. He wore the dungarees we'd seen him wear all month; the two of us dressed to the nines. He was energetic, affable—but most of all, and in a way that's impossible to overstate, he was serious. Where other writers would have rested on their laurels, he was busy lobbying for his present project—an opera. He was no good at small talk, too abrupt; he was busy all night long. This helps explain his torrential outpouring those years: he did not stop. His first question to me, always, was "What are you working on?" *October Light* was finished, therefore irrelevant.

The occasion was a success. There were important and beautiful people, good speeches and fine wines. At night's end we repaired to the Algonquin, where they nearly refused him a bed. He had a typewriter and briefcase as luggage, no credit cards or cash. We somehow convinced the desk clerk that Alfred Knopf himself would foot the bill, and were escorted to the suite. There were flowers and fruit, bottles waiting on ice; we ordered brandy as well. As the bellhop left, John sat. The couch was vast. He sank into its plush lushness, and mice scrambled from beneath his feet.

They were gone quickly; they scurried to some other section of the room. But in that first instant I thought they had emerged from his boots. We laughed. We placated Elena and informed the bellhop on his return that he should make certain hereafter to clear away the cheese. Yet the image remains and retains its first power to shock: I saw his power in the process of collapse. The telephone rang. At home he would answer, "Hello, Gardners'." That was, he explained, a way of being noncommittal; it was a large family, and you never knew which one the caller intended. It was also a way of keeping celebrity seekers at bay; he didn't have to say, "John Gardner" and could therefore always say he wasn't in. It rang again. He answered, "Hello, Gardner." He seemed forlorn; the brandy and Book Critics Circle had no power to invigorate. He was white and tired and, for all our efforts at support, alone.

Within the year, he was operated on for cancer. His first marriage had ended; his second—to a Bennington graduate, the poet L. M. Rosenberg—was in the offing, and he had moved from Vermont. They took him to Johns Hopkins Medical Center for emergency surgery; on Christmas I flew down. At dawn on Christmas Day the airports are deserted, so I had an empty, easy flight and arrived in Baltimore by nine.

He had not expected me and was watching television. His usual pallor was more pronounced still and made the bedsheet seem colorful. When he saw me, he blushed. It was, I teased him, the first and only time he'd been caught in the act of watching TV; James Page, the protagonist of John's *October Light*, had shot out the television screen in his house. So it would have been not pleasure but embarrassment that caused him to flush—but it was all right, I assured him, his secret addiction was safe. I blathered on like that until we felt at ease with silence; against hospital rules, he lit his pipe; all was well. I presented Christmas tokens; he complained about the trouble he was having with a paragraph; he had worked at it for three days now, but it wasn't right. The medicine tray held his IBM Selectric typewriter, and the windowsill was heaped with erasable bond. (The next time I visited him at Hopkins, he was sitting up in bed and busily at work—irritable, almost, at the interruption. The third time Elena came too, and we could not find him; he was in the reaches of the hospital basement, having commandeered a Xerox machine. But that first instant when I watched him through the open door remains the image here.) I knew— to see him reaching for the TV remote control and then for his pipe, turning even this cell into a work space, disorderly—he would survive.

His work will. Novelist, poet, critic, playwright, librettist, scholar, translator, fabulist—at forty-nine years old, he had the exuberance and protean energy of men not half his age. He was involved in the theater, in music, woodworking, publishing, teaching, painting—any number of pursuits and none of them casual or slapdash. His paintings were intensely seen; his boxes and furniture served. I remember dropping by his house in Bennington to find so many bookshelves fabricated in one day that I thought the pipe smoke in which he stood wreathed had caused my eyes to blur. He did seem, somehow, multiple. The first musical selection of the memorial service on East Main Street in Batavia—the town in upstate New York where he was born and buried—was a cassette of John and his son Joel, performing on their French horns. They played "Amazing Grace."

. . . .

This from Harry Percy's dying speech in *Henry IV, Part I*. Hotspur has been bested by his opposite, Prince Hal, and as he falls he prophesies:

> Oh, Harry, thou hast robbed me of my youth!
> I better brook the loss of brittle life
> Than those proud titles thou hast won of me.
> They wound my thoughts worse than thy sword my flesh.
> But thoughts, the slaves of life, and life, time's fool,
> And time that takes survey of all the world
> Must have a stop. . . .[1]

In the final thirty-eight words of this speech, there's only one ("survey") of more than a single syllable. Here as elsewhere, Shakespeare mimes the panting, hard-earned breath of someone who has little left, and there's nothing dull or monotonal about such bare-bones usage: "They wound my thoughts worse than thy sword my flesh. But thoughts, the slaves of life, and life, time's fool, and time that takes *survey* of all the word/Must have a stop."

In *Hamlet*, to take another example, the dying prince speaks in a similar vein. He goes from the polysyllabic Latinate utterance to the guttural Anglo-Saxon while the poison in his system does its lethal work: "Absent thee from felicity a while/And in this harsh world draw thy breath in pain." Felicity, for that melancholy Renaissance intellectual, is death, and to embrace absentia is to refrain from suicide; to survive and "tell my story" is to draw breath in pain. Hamlet's final line, of course, beggars any other sentence about our last condition; it's quite literally the last word: "The rest is silence."[2]

One of the comforts such lines can provide is a sense of ratification, a sense of commonality: X put it this way, Y understood just what I'm thinking, Z names the emotions I feel. What we recognize as familiar or, more formally, consonant with our own experience may in turn engender it; we can identify the emotion at hand because it's been described. Perhaps this is more true for writers than, say, real estate brokers or window washers, but I think it true for all humanity; we *are* what we have, in the oral-formulaic tradition, *heard* until we've memorized it; we are, in this literate age, at least in part what we've read.

In most ways this works to our bookish credit, but there's one quasi-comic disadvantage and obvious debit entailed. "Death" has long been a principal subject, a featured player—endemic to, epidemic in amateur texts. I mean by this that, though it's as certain as life, and all of us are born to die, it sometimes seems as though death plays a greater part in art than in the nature it mirrors. A good way of getting rid of a character is to kill him or her off.

In my undergraduate prose fiction class this semester, the carnage was general early on: a corpse per page. When I protested to my students that far fewer of them had seen a dead body than described one, they adduced the spectacle of movies and TV. By comparison with the celluloid mayhem of *Pulp Fiction*, for example, their own fictive attempts at slaughter were positively restrained. But think of all those extended death rattles, those characters on stage and in the opera house who spend an inordinate time dying in rhyme or tune, and the point seems evident: there's more metaphysics than physics, more metaphor than observation at work. Death is not uniformly violent, but neither is it a gentle good night, an imperceptible boundary crossing while eyelids flutter, then fall. As Dr. Sherman Nuland notes in his study, *How We Die*, the "death with dignity" we hope for is less a bodily than a spiritual condition; the patient will be convulsive as often as inert.

More generally, euphemism is the hallmark of our discourse on death. "He passed on," "she passed," "they went" or "departed" are common circumlocutories; catachresis—the rhetorical device of avoidance—holds the field. And though writers may use metaphor ("shuffled off this mortal coil") or abstraction ("that undiscovered country from whose bourne no traveler returns"), they by and large invite us to call a spade a spade. So when we "buy the farm" or "go the whole nine yards" or "push up daisies" or whatever, we indulge in graveyard referents: "ashes to ashes, dust dust."

The "death of little Nell" is a tearjerker at least in part because of the adjective, "little"; the death of "large" or "ancient Nell" would have had no such effect. It's "young" Patroclus or Juliet whose untimely passing we lament; old Priam or Lear arouses a different sort of rage and fear—a general lamentation as to the way of the world. When the elderly die at the end of the day, what we wish for them is peace; when a youthful protagonist dies, it's not so simple to be reconciled. The elegy is, more often than not, engendered by shock—a grievance that we work our way through with words. That form of lyric grief has returned of late, and even to a civilization with greatly increased actuarial life expectancy, because of the plague of AIDS. It's not an accident that in our present texts we once again die young.

"In my nineteenth year the darkness drew me down. And ah, the sweet sun." (This from the *Greek Anthology*, in a translation by Dudley Fitts.) My own favorite from that collection comes from the *Epitaph for a Sailor Lost at Sea:* "This gravestone lies if it says that it marks the place of my burial."[3]

Or think of a stanza in Thomas Nashe's fierce poem, "In Time of Pestilence," dated 1593:

> Beauty is but a flower
> Which wrinkles will devour;
> Brightness falls from the air;
> Queens have died young and fair;
> Dust hath closed Helen's eye
> I am sick, I must die.
> *Lord, have mercy on us!*[4]

More than half my life ago, I was a near neighbor of James Baldwin. We'd met in the winter of 1970, briefly, in Istanbul. I had been working on the screenplay for the film of my first novel, and the director knew Baldwin, and Baldwin was in town. We had a drink together and went to *Fortune and Men's Eyes*, a play of his translated into Turkish. Not knowing Turkish, I was less than enthralled, and the meeting did not matter much and the evening was a blur. The next year, however, my wife and I moved to the south of France, and we ran into Baldwin in Cannes. Standing on line at the American Express office, in what seemed like an interminable wait, I recognized Jimmy behind me. We shook hands. Then I said that the director who had introduced us would be passing through, and maybe we could get together for a meal or drink.

I was surprised, I think, at his alacrity; he invited us the next day. Elena's daybook for our final ten days in Provence lists five such occasions: dinner at his house, at ours, at a restaurant in Saint-Paul-de-Vence; and many talks and walks. He was completing *No Name in the Street;* he was planning to remain in France and would do so for years. His openhanded welcome, his insistence that we call as soon as we came back meant much, as did his cheerful certainty that we would return.

In 1973, when we settled again in the house in Provence, Baldwin treated us like long-lost friends. He had established a work pattern and an entourage. He had a chauffeur large enough to double as a bodyguard, a cook, a companion named Philippe who acted as a kind of secretary-manager, and various others whose function is less easy to describe. There would be a dancer or painter in attendance—old lovers or associates from some project in the offing, or projected, or long past. They came from Italy, America, Algeria, Tunisia, Finland. Brothers and nephews passed through.

We were rarely fewer than six at table, and more often ten. The cook and the *femme de ménage* came and went; the men stayed on. They treated their provider with a fond deference, as if his talent must be sheltered from invasive detail, the rude importunate matters of fact. They answered the phone and the door. They sorted mail. There was an intricate hierarchy of rank, a jockeying for position that evoked nothing so much as a Provençal court—who was in favor, who out, who had known Jimmy longer or better or where, who would do the shopping or join him in Paris for the television interview or help with the book jacket photo. He was working, again, on a novel: *If Beale Street Could Talk.*

Baldwin drank scotch. We drank wine. I have not yet described the quality of kindness in his manner, the affection he expected and expressed. His face is widely known—that dark glare, broad nose, those large protruding eyes, the close-fitting cap of curls then starting to go white. But photographs cannot convey the mobile play of features, the intensity of utterance, the sense he could contrive to give that attention *matters* and gesture can count. There was something theatrical in Jimmy's manner, and it grew automatic at times. He would embark on what seemed a tirade, a high-speed compilation of phrases that clearly had been phrased before, a kind of improvised lecture spun out of previous speech. He stared at you unblinkingly; you could not turn away. He wore expensive jewelry and fingered it, talking; he smoked. He had been holding center stage for years.

You shifted in your seat. You said, "Yes, but . . ." and he raised his imperious manicured hand. Dialogue, for Baldwin, was an interrupted monologue; he would yield the platform neither willingly nor long. He could speak incisively on a book he had not read. But again and again he impressed me with his canny ranging, his alert intelligence. "Understand me," he would say. "It's important you understand." And it *was* important, and in that mesmeric presence you thought you understood. . . .

My pleasure in our meetings is easily explained. Here was the spokesman of his generation and color, speaking directly to me. That he took my opinions seriously; that he read and respected my work, or appeared to; that he wanted us with him as often as possible—all this was flattering. When we parted late at night, Jimmy would say, "See you two tomorrow." If we came for lunch instead, he would urge us to stay on for dinner; when a friend passed through Saint-Paul, he would insist we meet.

Why he wanted to spend time with us is, I think, less clear. Each friendship partakes of the reciprocal trade agreement, and I can only speculate as to Baldwin's motives in the exchange. He was the most sociable of solitaries; though constantly attended and attended to, he held himself apart.

He wanted to hear "news from home." Elena had worked several years in a rehabilitation agency for drug addicts in New York, whose clientele was largely black; she moved easily through his old streets. Though she was without exception the sole woman in his house—and in a party of, often, as many as a dozen men—she was given pride of place. She sat at his right hand. They liked each other, I believe, with unfettered immediate liking; she treated him with just the right mixture of impatience and respect. They embraced each other, meaning it; they huddled in corners together. There was nothing exclusionary about his attitude to women; though surrounded by adoring boys, he was also a "family man."

I mattered to him, I suppose, as a practitioner of a shared trade. He told me he was starved for the chance to talk books, for a discussion, say, of Henry James with someone who had read him. We talked the way most writers do, in a kind of shorthand and sign language. We asked each other, always, how the work had gone that day, how this paragraph was doing, or that character and scene. . . .

Jimmy's acolytes believed the process sacramental, as if behind his study door strange rituals took place. He would shut himself away at midnight and somehow produce an object to which accrued money and fame. They had little sense, I think, of how much it was costing him to keep them all in style, of the anxious private wrangling in the watches of the night. His acclaim had diminished of late, and he knew I knew it. The alchemy of which his friends were confident was less mysterious to me and therefore more compelling; he worked at continual risk. And I was moved by his intensity, his struggle with a form that had come to seem elusive. *Beale Street* is not as finely honed as *Go Tell It on the Mountain* or *Giovanni's Room*. Yet writers must begin anew each time they start to write. That Baldwin had been consequential to a multitude of readers made all of this more poignant; he had made himself the benchmark to be passed.

Much of what I knew of the plight of the black American I had learned from reading him. And what sometimes seemed like paranoia could be argued as flat fact. The deaths of Malcolm X, of Medgar Evers, Martin Luther King Jr., Bobby Kennedy, George Jackson, the named and nameless legion in what he called "the royal fellowship of death"; his own impending fiftieth birthday; the sickness of a beloved friend and mentor, the painter Beauford Delaney—all weighed heavily that winter. "This face," he'd say, and frame it with his slender glinting fingers. "Look at this crazy face."

In the early 1970s Richard Nixon reigned unchallenged. The Watergate scandal was building, but the hearings had not yet begun. Each day brought more darkness to light. One litmus test for national allegiance, perhaps, has to do with political scandal; the French took corruption for granted, but we were transfixed. We rushed out for the paper and listened to the radio daily, but a "smoking gun" or upheaval in the political affairs of France could trigger no equivalent concern.

We waited like literal exiles for the summons to return. We discussed America with the fervor of the unrequited lover, curdling into scorn. We went for walks; we dawdled over drinks; we visited each other ("Hey, baby, what's up?" "Hey, darlin', where've you *been*?") often and often those months.

Elena and I had been at his house in Saint-Paul-de-Vence two or three times in a row; it was our turn, therefore, to invite the Baldwin clan. We did so, one Thursday, for lunch. They said they would come, happily; they were seven, maybe nine. The two members of his party I remember as men passing through were a dancer called Bertrand and a publisher named Willi. The former was lean, lithe, beautiful, and black; he danced at the Folies-Bergère. The latter was mountainous, white. We had been warned about his appetite by Baldwin's cook days before; Willi was a voracious eater who had sent her to the market three times that afternoon.

Elena planned a *navarin*; we made an extra pot. A *navarin*, though simple, takes time to prepare; we started the previous day. We peeled turnips and carrots and leeks. We cubed the lamb and browned it, then fashioned the *bouquet garni*. Our landlady knocked. She was hoping we might join her tomorrow for lunch; she'd asked people she thought we should meet. Lilo Rosenthal was eighty years old; she owned the property of which we occupied the gatehouse, and she was being generous to her youthful tenants. But we made our excuses, inviting her in; as she could see, we too were preparing a meal. We would therefore be unable to join or invite her, for we owed a friend a thank-you *navarin*. I remember not naming his name. Part of this was inverse snobbery, a distaste for glitter by association, and part the suspicion that, had Lilo known Baldwin was coming, we should have had to invite her also. They would have been water and oil.

At any rate, she told us, she hoped we would take in our wash. It hung on the clothesline outside. She intended to walk by the house and let her friends take photographs; they were passionate photographers. Her friends were distinguished, she said. They were the last of the Hapsburgs and the last of the Hohenzollerns, respectively. Or perhaps they were the last of the Schleswigs and Holsteins, or collateral branches instead. In any case, they were old and distinguished and would not appreciate the laundry on our line. She hoped we would ready the house.

We promised. We made the second *navarin*, brought an extra dozen bottles from the *cave*, bought three additional *boules* from the baker, and waited for Jimmy to come. He himself did not drive. He had, however, purchased a brand-new Mercedes, dark brown and substantial, just short of stretch-limousine size. His driver would be working that day, he had assured me, and he was bringing Bertrand, Daro, Philippe, Billy, Willi, and Bernard.

At the appointed hour we were ready; a car came. The day was overcast. What pulled into the parking space between our gatehouse and the villa was not Jimmy's Mercedes but an ancient gray Renault. It was followed, funereally, by a Deux Chevaux. Lilo Rosenthal appeared. Her guests emerged. They were slow and small and bent. The process of arrival took some time. The doors opened, faltered, closed. The last of the Hapsburgs and the last of the Hohenzollerns wore dark suits and carried cameras and advanced with umbrellas and canes. They shuffled off together to their hostess's house.

As soon as they were out of sight, we heard another car. The deep-throated growl of gears, the high hum of power in harness, the trumpeting bravura of the horn—and Baldwin's Mercedes roared up. It spat the raked gravel; it rocked on its brakes; it fairly pirouetted in the sudden sun. Four doors flung wide in unison; our company had come!

They were dressed for the occasion, grandly. They wore boaters and foulards. Their boots gleamed. Bertrand especially was splendid; he emerged twirling his scarf and waist sash of pink silk. He did a few dance steps and flung his hat high and extended his hands for applause. We applauded. Jimmy embraced us; we him. The chauffeur was not happy with the switchbacks of the entry drive. "They're badly banked," he said. He had brought his lunch along and elected to stay with the car. He stood, arms folded, glowering down through the olive groves; he was Danish, thick and stolid and impervious to charm. "What a charming place," the publisher proclaimed. We piloted them in.

This was not easy. They swarmed. They raced to the crest of the meadow and walked tiptoe along the rim of the irrigating cistern that doubled as a pool. They approved the view. They clattered through our little house, exclaiming at the style of it, posing on the bedroom balcony. "Give me the simple life," they chorused. "Let's have *la vie en rose*." Philippe had brought flowers; he garlanded Elena, Daro, Jimmy, Willi, and Bertrand. We emptied four bottles of wine by the time we settled to eat.

The *navarin* was a success. The publisher, Willi, approved. Audibly, he sighed, sitting back on the banquette and rolling up his sleeves. "Which pot's for me?" he asked. There were olives and pâté. There was much laughter, celebration, praise for the salads and bread. The dining room could barely contain us; we rolled about the table like a litter of puppies suckling, jostling, slicing sausages and cheese and fruit and cake. A shadow appeared at the window. I looked up. Lilo Rosenthal was outside by the car. She and her four companions were

inching toward the house. They had their cameras at shoulder
level, focusing, and it pained them, clearly, to approach.

We must have looked, to them, like Spengler's nightmare
realized: the decline of the West. The beaming black man at
the center, the lithe array around him, the voluminous white
man with loaves in his hands, the young hosts plying everyone with wine, the pyramid of bottles, the ruckus of festivi-
ty, the Mercedes being polished—all this was hard to focus
on or frame. I could see Lilo explaining. I do not know how
she explained. There was no laundry, however. They circled
warily. We did not invite them in. They moved to the back
of the house.

One organizing principle of realism is that we mirror nature,
and by doing so reflect as well as reflect upon it. We engage
in selective verbal imitation of the world beyond the word. A
phrase from literary criticism may bring these lines full circle, since writers like to identify and then avoid "the fallacy
of imitative form." This means, for all practical purposes,
that one shouldn't write about boring people boringly, about
brilliant conversation brilliantly, or death in deathly prose.
Yet whatever one says about death is by definition provi-
sional, and to describe it authoritatively as author is to con-
struct a fiction. We write of "morbid matters" obsessively
and know nothing about them at all.

Many who might read these lines will, I imagine, have
witnessed the dead; some may have witnessed the passing of
life; a few indeed may have taken it—and, with rifle or anti-
aircraft gun, killed. Yet none of us *knows* death except by observation or perhaps deduction; to have experienced it at first
hand is to complete one's career.

That other universal experience, birth, is scarcely more familiar; we've forgotten what it felt like, surely, by the time we
sit to write. As E. M. Forster put it, in his *Aspects of the Novel:*

Our final experience, like our first, is conjectural. We move
between two darknesses. Certain people pretend to tell us

what birth and death are like: a mother, for instance, has her point of view about birth; a doctor, a religious, have their points of view about both. But it is all from the outside, and the two entities who might enlighten us, the baby and the corpse, cannot do so, because their apparatus for communicating their experiences is not attuned to our apparatus for reception. . . . So let us think of people as starting life with an experience they forget and ending it with one which they anticipate but cannot understand.[5]

Tolstoi claimed to remember the womb, and perhaps he did, but few lesser mortals can persuasively argue the same. I've not done a statistical analysis nor asked a computer to make such a search, but it's my anecdotal impression that much less language has in fact been allocated to the beginning of life than to its end. On a greeting-card rack there's more space devoted to "the new arrival," weddings and birthdays and "get better soon" cards, than "sympathy" or death; in "serious" literature, however, the reverse seems more nearly the case. "Every third thought," as Prospero declares while he and his author announce their retirement, "shall be my grave." This proportion may be overstated, but it's not over-far from the literary mark.

The *Oxford Dictionary of Quotations* has more than a full index page of such allusions. I admire the space-saving device that reduces the referenced word to its first letter and a period. So "death"—to take only the opening examples from the alphabet's first letter—is central to such phrases as "After the first d.," "All in the valley of D.," "allotted d. and hell," "Any man's d. diminishes," "apprehends d. no more dreadfully," and "arms of cool-enfolding d." The authors of these peculiar assertions are, in order, the poets Dylan Thomas ("After the first death"), Alfred Lord Tennyson ("All in the valley of Death"), Christopher Marlowe ("allotted death and hell"), John Donne ("Any man's death diminishes me"), William Shakespeare ("apprehends death no more dreadfully") and Walt Whitman ("arms of cool-enfolding death"). To cite such a company, not to mention the several hundred other referents in any such book of quotations, is to acknowledge how often and how well all this has been addressed: whatever the risks and temptations of imitative form, we have an oxymoronic compulsion to write in lively fashion about the lack of life.

One comfort that attaches to the profession has to do with this act of completion; writers can have the last word. Yeats planned for his own tombstone the conclusion of his poem, "Under Ben Bulben":

> On limestone quarried near the spot
> By his command these words are cut:
> Cast a cold eye
> On life, on death.
> *Horseman, pass by!*[6]

Goethe was a touch more runic and less resolute. His dying remark was the German, *"Mehr licht"*—"More light"—a phrase evoking the Enlightenment he had done so much to foster, and the great man's restive—Faustian—intellectual questing. My own guess is he was shouting at the chambermaid, telling her to bring another candle or lantern to his bed. Of these my favorite is Admiral Nelson's, "Kiss me, Hardy." The admiral was, by all accounts, very conscious of his place in history and—because he was at perpetual risk in battle—had prepared his final words. They were to be "Kismet, Hardy," a resigned and soldierly acknowledgment of the hand of *kismet*, fate. But according to this story, in the din of the Battle of Trafalgar, the great guns going off, the smoke and shouting everywhere, what Hardy his valet heard was "Kiss me, Hardy." I love to imagine that great leering face as the last thing Nelson saw, all blood-spattered and bewhiskered, saying, "I didn't know you felt that way about me, Guvnor; 'ere, let's 'ave a little kiss. . . ."

And, finally, a poem from Constantin Cavafy:

LONG AGO

I'd like to speak of this memory . . .
but it's so faded now . . . as though nothing is left—
because it was so long ago, in my early adolescent years.

A skin as though of jasmine . . .
that August evening—was it August?—
I can still just recall the eyes: blue, I think they were . . .
Ah yes, blue; a sapphire blue.

(Translated by Edmund Keeley and Philip Sherrard)[7]

One hot summer morning in Paris I woke with my mouth full of blood. I was very young—eighteen—and this was very long ago and I was frightened, alone. Well, not alone entirely; in the next room of our cheap hotel on the Rue des Écoles a friend of mine was sleeping with a friend of his, a Dutch girl he'd courted the previous night, and they were busy in bed. The sounds they made quieted mine. I coughed and hawked into a handkerchief and watched it turn bright red. Even then I hoped to be a writer, and I knew the letter where Keats claimed that, as a medical man, he could recognize his own arterial blood and knew it to be a death sentence; the lines with which the poet predicted his extinction were ones I'd learned by heart.

But I myself could barely tell the measles from the mumps. Except for this strange bubbling redness at my lips, I felt fine that morning; I would have liked to gargle, would have liked to brush my teeth, but the sink was in the couple's room and, until they finished their coupling, it seemed impolite to intrude. It wasn't—I rubbed it—my tongue. It wasn't a cut on my cheek or my gums, and the uncertainty (consumption? a collapsed lung or ruptured aorta? some disease that leveled brilliant youth?) was, in its own way, romantic. I returned to the book by my bed.

That summer I was reading—*everybody* was, or so it seemed—*The Alexandria Quartet*. Lawrence Durrell's word-drunk panegyric to the charms of dissolution and the "poet of the city" had introduced me to Cavafy; "the soft bloom of phthisis," for example, was a phrase I planned to use soon. The dark outskirts of Paris where wolves ran freely in the time of plague was known to Villon as "Le Louvre"; I planned to use that too. And I had fallen in love with *Clea*, or the idea of her, the name and image and book about her. So I spat in my wine glass and read.

The bleeding continued; the procedure next door did not. I rose and knocked and frothily informed my friend that I was coughing blood and might need to find a doctor and did he know one, or—since she'd said the night before that she'd been in town since Tuesday—did the girl? I cannot remember her name. She looked at me with interest, a new-kindled glint in her blue-eyed gaze, and then I remembered a family acquaintance, a man my parents had urged me to call who lived on the Right Bank and would surely have a doctor. He did; he gave me a telephone number and told me to proceed there *immédiatement;* I must take a taxi. He would pay.

And so I drove across Paris like a modern-day, better-heeled Rimbaud or Keats, composing my own epitaph and fetching up at last at the provided address. The doctor's office was capacious; there was art on the walls and jasmine blooming in a vase and an elegant, middle-aged nurse who told me to sit down and wait. Coughing, hawking, spitting, I obliged. By the time *Monsieur le Mèdecin* examined me, there was no blood, no single bloom of phthisis left, and he explained in pidgin English that I had burst a little, a *very* little capillary in my tonsils and—he spread his hands and, smiling, shrugged—this history was over now and nothing to fear.

My friend is dead; Durrell is dead; Cavafy himself had died in 1933. I never saw that naked girl again and it was Paris in July, not Alexandria in August—was it August? Deprived of my romance, I left, walking slowly back to the Rue des Écoles. Carrion comfort for the plebe of words: this would make a story someday.

An Old Man Mad About Writing

Ford Madox Ford's last published book is an important one. Though little read and rarely discussed, *The March of Literature* holds a mirror to the artist's nature as he examines the nature of art. Like all critical assessments of the work of others, this text reveals at least as much about the critic who does the assessing; few road maps of an author's aesthetic will chart terrain so closely as the map he or she draws. While it purports to objectivity, *The March of Literature* is an intensely personal work, a kind of swan song as trumpet voluntary, advancing the case for language as civilization's main prop. Undertaken in his sixties, researched and composed during a period of heart attacks and rheumatism so severe he claimed he could not dress himself or even brush his hair, this survey subtitled *From Confucius' Day to Our Own* is vintage Ford; no one else could have produced it or would, perhaps, have tried.

Nor did he disguise the idiosyncratic aspect of his enterprise; several pages of quotation are given to Spanish picaresque tales, nearly none to Shakespeare's plays. The editors made cuts and changes without authorial permission; what Ford wrote is not verbatim what we read. When published in 1938 by The Dial Press, *The March of Literature* sold poorly, and it was long out of print. Like those other encyclopedic ventures, *The Outline of History* by H. G. Wells and Will Durant's *Story of Philosophy*, it has the feel of a period piece. There are inaccuracies and excesses throughout. Yet I think it a splendid performance, 850 pages chock-a-block with information, a passionately embraced espousal of what that devotee of writing found humane and sane.

Some twenty years ago, I published *Group Portrait: Conrad, Crane, Ford, James, & Wells*. It is a biographical study of writers in community, its thesis that colleagueship matters, and it was in large part powered by a desire to celebrate Ford Madox Ford. His sense of a community of letters—the debt artists owe one another, the way to discharge that debt openhandedly, the quasi-medieval notion of apprenticeship that must earn walking papers on the road to mastery—seemed to me impressive. Exemplary, even, in his glad willingness to praise both seniors and juniors, sponsors and detractors, his unswerving commitment to the enterprise of art. I was and am moved by the figure of Ford—his offhand erudition and editorial acumen, his skill with spade and frying pan, the way he seemed at equal ease in evening clothes and a gardener's smock. That shambling elegance, the "small producer's" voluminous output, the rooted rootlessness: all compelled me then and continue to do so today. As V. S. Pritchett wrote in *The Working Novelist:* "He was nature's expatriate, his country was the Novel, he left his baggage in every hotel room."[1]

Writers need no blood relation in order to trace ancestry, and this sort of influence depends on no family tree. Through the good office of a bookshelf, apprenticeship enlarges; we may claim close acquaintance with those we've never met. Young Ford himself lodged such a claim, though his own chosen models (Bertran de Born and François Villon, for instance) could not drop by for drinks. The youthful artist did collaborate with Conrad on a book called *The Inheritors*, and inheritance is multiform; why not acknowledge indebtedness or an indirect line of descent?

So now that I approach the age of Ford in his last years, I want to celebrate instead the work of "an old man mad about writing." This phrase was a cap-tip to Hokusai, who called himself "an old man mad about painting," and our author used the line often. The self-aggrandizing self-denigration ("old man"), the monosyllabic colloquial ("mad")—by which he meant, of course, "infatuated" as well as "angry" or "insane"—the generic abstraction ("painting" or "writing"), the casual referent to a great predecessor—all compressed into eight syllables and resulting in a vivid epithet: one understands why Ford was fond of it. The phrase can be found, for instance, in the preface to *The March of Literature*, written almost a half century after his first foray into print. "It is the book of an old man mad about writing—in the sense that Hokusai called himself an old man mad about painting. So it is an attempt to induce a larger and always larger number of my fellows to taste the pleasure that comes from always more and more reading."[2]

To start with, therefore, Ford posits a linkage between "writing" and "reading"; the one requires the other and "pleasure" derives "always more and more" from both. As he puts it a few pages later:

> Let us then sum up Literature as that which men read and continue to read for pleasure or to obtain that imaginative culture which is necessary for civilizations. Its general characteristic is that it is the product of a poetic, an imaginative, or even merely a quaintly observant mind. Since the days of Confucius, or the earliest Egyptian writers a thousand years before his time, there have been written in stone, on papyrus, wax, vellum, or merely paper, an immense body of matter—innumerable thousands of tons of it.[3]

The March of Literature presents a kind of inventory of those "thousands of tons," and its quasi-military title entails the forward motion suggested by a march. Its author described his massive volume as a survey of world literature, beginning with the Egyptians, the Old Testament, Xenophon, and Confucius and ending with Flaubert and Conrad, Turgenev, and Dostoevski. Such groupings argue continuity; the late and great and recent were part of a party of wordsmiths for whom Ford served as host.

This project appears to have been one he contemplated for years, and by 1937 the time was finally ripe. A recent biographer, Alan Judd, describes the work's inception:

(Allen) Tate had met Joseph Brewer, the new President of Olivet College, Michigan, at a writer's conference. Brewer, who had a publishing background and was keen to further the cause of all the arts at Olivet . . . was already an admirer of Ford's writing and proposed to offer him the post of writer and critic in residence. Allen Tate, Brewer and Ford met in New York that winter and agreed (on) a salary of $1500 with an additional fee of $150 for Ford's attending the Olivet Writers' Conference during the summer of 1937. Ford was to spend about eight months of the year in residence, talking about literature with those who wanted to talk, reading, writing and generally being man of letters to the campus. It was not quite a living wage but it was near enough and the recognition was probably as important as the money.

The other benefit of that December in New York was that he was able to interest the Dial Press in his long-cherished project of writing a history of world literature. This was to become *The March of Literature,* his last great task and a truly Herculean one. His description of it as a survey from Confucius to Conrad is not an exaggeration and he read or reread every book or author it deals with, often in the original. Coinciding with the Olivet offer, he knew now that he would have a safe base from which to work, a measure of security and a library on which to draw freely; in other words, a little, at last, of what most who have written about him have taken for granted throughout their working lives.[4]

Olivet, Michigan, lies twenty miles or so northeast of Battle Creek and thirty south of Lansing. It's a little town—a

village, truly—surrounded by large farms. Main Street is sig-
naled by a stop sign, not a traffic light, and the WELCOME
sign at the town limit boasts that Olivet was home of the 1990
Class "C" Girls Cross Country State Champions. There's a
car wash and a Taco Bell and a drive-through bank, yet it
must look much the same today as when Ford arrived some
sixty-five years ago, with Janice Biala, and stayed. The car
wash and the restaurant are recent additions, of course, and
Olivet College has modestly expanded; there's a gymnasium,
a student center, and a child-care playground back behind the
church. But the Olivet City Cemetery borders the small campus still; unprepossessing houses cluster on the grid of
streets, and what's expansive is the sky. Ford and Janice had
a "tiny house, not much bigger than a hen coop" (according
to Robie Macauley) and Lord knows how they stocked it
with or where they purchased those indispensables, olive oil,
garlic, and wine. When writing such books as *The Cinque
Ports* or *Provence*, Ford memorialized the "heart of the country" and called himself "an extremely dirty agricultural la-
borer," yet this is small town life with a vengeance; it's hard
to imagine anywhere less promising for a citizen of London,
Paris, and New York to have settled in and stayed.

Settle in and down he did, however, and though he complained of the weather—the summer heat, the winter chill—
he never disparaged the place. The supportive welcome of
Olivet's president, Joseph Brewer, was palpably pleasing to
Ford. When in 1938 he received an honorary degree from
the school, he could scarcely contain his delight. In the description Arthur Mizener gives of the event, the honoree
"provided characteristically inventive material for the cita-
tion; Professor Akley, the college orator, found himself
telling the assembled company that Ford was 'a Dr. of Agri-
culture of the University of Sorbonne,' that he had 'known
war as a colonel in charge of two regiments in action,' that
he had been the 'first to praise Dreiser in England, first to
credit Joyce and Stein . . . first to publish a short story by
Arnold Bennett and by Galsworthy' and was the 'guarantor
of Conrad's first novel, Almayer's Folly.'"[5] We need not

credit Mizener's habitual disapproval; there's a photo of the honoree and Dr. Brewer being jolly together in academic robes, and for the occasion our Doctor of Letters purchased a new three-piece suit. "A Man Could Stand Up" here, clearly, and bring the wretched heathen to the light.

In his dedicatory epistle to *The March of Literature*, Ford makes explicit his indebtedness. This from "A Dedication Which is Also an Author's Introduction" to Joseph Hillyer Brewer and Robert Greenlees Ramsay, President and Dean of Men, Olivet College, Michigan:

> So you set up your educational institution in which the professoriate consists solely of practicing artists—amongst whom it was my pride to enroll myself and my pleasure to serve. And having, thus, your corporate assurance that I was an artist, I thought I might undertake this book.[6]

The new member of the faculty had a lifelong reverence for learning—his father and the much-admired Arthur Marwood were university men—yet this was his first foray into academe. Writers take its patronage for granted now, but at that time the notion of an "artist in residence" was new. Brewer was a forward-facing patron, and he seems to have asked of Ford nothing more formal than his presence: being a genius, striding up and down the Olivet green, perorating to what must have been astonished students on the work of words. To some degree *The March of Literature* seems a companion text to those instructive rambles; at Olivet Ford was professing what for decades he had preached.

He cherished the conviction, for example, that the only true civilization was "a Latin—a Mediterranean—civilization (that) has a definite place for the providers of literature," and this preference is manifest throughout:

> A Cicero can mould the fortunes of an empire, a Lamartine those of a republic; the lightest word of a Victor Hugo will travel to the ear of the remotest peasant in the land. . . . A member of the French Academy has the precedence of a

Marshal of France, and all the garrisons of France must turn
out to salute him as he passes by. . . . But . . . look at any time
in one or other half of Anglo-Saxondom and you will find
our best writers starving.[7]

Or, again:

When you have said the names of the *Odyssey,* of the Bible,
of *Oedipus Tyrannus,* of the *Divine Comedy* itself and the
great and little testaments of Villon you have almost ex-
hausted the catalogue of the great . . . works of humanity. . . . You might, if you liked, add Rabelais.[8]

While discussing Virgil and the Latin poets, he avers:

To parody Caesar, we might well write: *Tota humanitas in
duas partes divisa est.* There are those who like their wines
neat and those who like synthetic alcohol flavored with rasp-
berry juice; there are those who seek in their books to meet
with *les émotions fortes* and those who consider, along with
the British Censor, that all art must be arranged so that it
shall not shock pregnant women. . . . It is, indeed, the difference between the mediaeval and the renaissance. And, es-
sentially, it is the difference between the ferocious rendering
of life by those who have lived or have at least speculated on
life and the rendering of stylized and expurgated manners by
those who have studied the others and know how to select
passages for imitation and tempered verbiage such as shall
not be injurious to our mothers before childbirth.[9]

And, finally:

The quality of literature, in short, is the quality of humanity.
It is the quality that communicates, between man and men, the
secret of human hearts and the story of our vicissitudes.[10]

The Olivet College Library has been renovated and enlarged. It's still a small building, however, and the metal steps

up through the stacks are no doubt those Ford maneuvered his bulk athwart and where he, wheezing, paused to check a source or add to his grab-bag of texts. In the old library's new reading room, a bronze bust of "J. H. Brewer, Educator" looks down benignly, hand on a book, and there are photographs of the first three graduates of Olivet in 1863: Miss Sophia A. Keyes, Miss Mary N. Barber, and Miss Sara Benedict.

Ford's office was in the library basement, and there he took tea and held forth, accumulating a thousand words a day. He had begun the book in Clarksville, Tennessee, with Robert Lowell and Allen and Carolyn Tate, dictating to Janice's sister-in-law, a Mrs. Jack Tworkov. Robert Lowell describes him as always having "armloads of Loeb classics." There's an intimate wrangling discursiveness here, as though the host of a party has buttonholed guests, and it's of no real consequence if they are distant or dead. As Robie Macauley remembers, "He succeeded in giving the impression, for instance, that though he had just missed meeting Marlowe in London, he knew all about him and was very much excited by the young man's work."[11]

Although organized chronologically, the book does feel digressive—chatty even, conversational—and this no doubt in part derives from its origins in speech. On the final forced march to completion, Ford started work at five in the morning and finished at seven at night. Years before, he had transcribed spoken utterance from Conrad, and Henry James made of dictation a routine procedure, yet it still beggars the imagination—beggars mine, at any rate—to think of anyone producing so much scholarship so fast. In the preface to his best-known work, *The Good Soldier*, Ford famously averred that, at forty, he wanted to show what he could do. Well past sixty when he undertook *The March of Literature*, he wanted to show what he knew.

What he knew was considerable. Let me list a sample of page headings in order to suggest the flavor of the whole: "The Hebrews in Bondage"; "Xenophon Lives the Anabasis"; "Cyrus and Croesus"; "The Subtle Rihaku"; "Kau-Tsu Founds the Tang Dynasty"; "The Vulgate and the Versio

Recepta"; "The Song of Solomon"; "Metrical Forms"; "Herodotus Projects the World of his Day"—and I've not even reached page 100. Later we have "Pisistratus Preserves Homer's Tales"; "Euripides Listens in the Market Place"; "The Archives of Alexandria"; "Pindar, Stesichorus and Alcman"; "Theocritus, Bion and Moschus"; "Oratory, the Primitive Newspaper"; "The Philippics"; "Aristotle, Seeker of Instances"; "Plotinus and his School"; "Catullus and Cockney Dialect"; "The Temperament of Propertius"; "Tibullus, Who Lived on a Farm." By page 200 Ford turns his attention to "The Verse of Horace"; "Virgil's Georgics"; "The Aeneid"; "The Imagination of Ovid"; and "The Tactlessness of Lucan" and proceeds apace, pausing for breath with Cicero and Caesar, bivouacking with the troubadours, sharing a campaign with Dante, and marshalling arms with "Bold Bertran de Born." There are pages on Chaucer and "The Orlando Furioso of Ariosto," studies of "Ronsard" and "Lyly, the Juggler of Words"; there are discussions of "Sacred Histrionics"; "German Folksongs"; "Meditations of a Friar"; "Donne's Impatience"; 'Marvell's Cavalier Indifference"; "The Procuress Celestina"; "The Picaresque Novel"; "Lazarillo de Tormes"; "Lessing"; "Corneille, Moliere and Racine." Let me turn now to a rapid survey of the final hundred: "Poor Théophile Gautier"; "Sainte-Beuve and Literary Criticism"; "Newspaperman Cobbett"; "Alfred Lord Tennyson"; "Austere Wordsworth"; "'I am Walt Whitman'"; "Stendahl's Dry, Direct Style"; "Jane Austen and Trollope"; "Sudermann, Hauptmann and Schnitzler"; "Hendrik Ibsen"; "The Enigmatic Mr. Dickens"; "Balzac's Tinny Rhythm," and by page 825, "We come then to Flaubert, Henry James and Joseph Conrad."

Here Ford celebrates again the virtues of impressionism, complains of "Publishers and Booksellers," proselytizes for "Ezra Pound" and "Crane's Red Badge of Courage"; the last page heading, on 849, is bravely—brazenly—enough, three words: "On Eternal Beauty."

I take this to be his clarion call. What he's after is enduringness, the true "distinguished thing." As he writes in praise of Chateaubriand, "Let then this writer and this reader take hands. Descending our hillside, let us jump the little brook of time and mingle with the great creatures who are browsing amongst the asphodels of those Elysian Fields."[12] The passage "On Eternal Beauty" refers, moreover, to the painter Delacroix and a journal entry from 1859. Ford considers it to be "astonishingly true as a comment on a history of literature" and translates it as follows:

> Real beauty is eternal and would be accepted at all periods; but it wears the dress of its century; something of that dress clings to it and woe to works which appear in periods when the general taste is corrupted.

Then the writer speculates on fashion, the Wheel of Fortune turning so that what went up comes down. It's hard not to note the wistfulness here, an anticipatory whiff of the tomb:

> Nevertheless, real beauty is eternal, the corruption of one generation's taste being the delight of generations hundreds of years in the future. The humorousnesses of Shakespeare and the bitternesses of Dante set on edge the teeth of the generations immediately succeeding each of them—because the humor was a hundred times twice told, and the bitternesses directed to dead men who, public parties changing, had become heroes. Today we ignore alike the witticisms and the reasons for the bitterness, as if both humor and bitterness were a little dust on the marble of the "Victory of Samothrace." So it may well be with this writer's dead friends and their great masters.[13]

Although he had insisted, a few pages previous, that "The main and perhaps most passionate tenet of impressionism was the suppression of the author from the pages of his books,"[14] nothing could be further from Ford's case. There's no suppression here, no authorial absence or disguise, and it takes a paragraph at most to identify our writer's characteristic note. His refrain: art matters, the well-chosen phrase, not the showy or the self-absorbed (as in his *bête noir*, Robert Louis Stevenson's "With interjected finger he delayed the action of the timepiece")[15] but the one that *makes you see*. Those periods and artists he believes were best at this include:

> the Greece of the Great Age, Rome of the Augustans, Arles of the troubadours, China of the second century, Italy of Dante, Petrarch and Boccacio, France of Villon and the Pleiade. . . . The main feature of these other great literatures and literary periods is that each is distinguished by one almost superhuman figure around which stand the other great grouped towers of cathedrals. So for China you would have Lao-Tsze; for the Hebrews, Isaiah; for the Greeks, Homer; for the Augustans, Horace; for the troubadours, Peire Vidal; for the French, Villon; for the Spaniards, Cervantes . . . and you can add as in the case of towns that boast more than one central spire, Confucius, Theocritus, Aeschylus, the psalmist Augustine, Ronsard. . . . A great company.[16]

It's worth noting how reluctant Ford is to include English names in the list. Elsewhere he will cite a few, but his heart is cross-channel, his admiration unstinting for those who border the Mediterranean or sail the Aegean, those who ply the great trade routes where the sun is fierce. And always he praises the passionate fancy, when yoked to self-control—by which he means a conscious artistry. That tension between passion and restraint is the engine of his work, its *primum mobile*. Between temptation and the cautionary "Some Do Not" is the mined landscape Ford traverses, the territory limned in both his creative and critical prose. From Edward Ashburnham and Katharine Howard to Christopher Tietjens, he drew portrait after portrait of the divided self, the moral man and woman beset by conflicting desires. And *The March of Literature* belongs to that same portrait gallery; it's another of his brave attempts to shape what seems disorderly and lend form to the inchoate: *In the beginning was the word.* . . .

Here's his beginning assertion, the gauntlet he throws down:

In the book that follows, we shall confine ourselves exclusively to chronicling the humaner letters of the world. If we succeed in turning out a work of insight and imagination and one couched in clear, uncomplicated and not harsh prose, we may make ourselves see the great stream of literature issuing from its dark and remote sources and broadening through the centuries until it comes to irrigate with its magnificent and shining waters, almost the whole of the universe of today. If we succeed in that, we too shall have produced . . . a piece of literature.[17]

He does succeed; he produced it. In this regard what moves me most is not the argument as such, not the bill of particulars but the general proclamation, the drumroll and loud call to arms: an inward-facing admonition to be *serious*. Who else could write with a straight face about "the great stream of literature . . . broadening through the centuries until it comes to irrigate with its magnificent and shining waters, almost the whole of the universe of today"? Who else would dive so trustfully into those shining waters and emerge, though rheumatic, refreshed? Eight hundred and forty-five pages later, Ford closes with a prophecy as to the art of the future, its irrepressible forward march: "Why, yes, it will come, because all those things have been put into the world by our art and because all the peoples of the earth demand nothing else, if only that they may have a little rest from their fears and the leisure to sit down and read. And what the Master shall command the hand of the slave shall contrive."[18]

Let Joseph Brewer have the last biographical word. In his "Ford Madox Ford: a Memoir," a tribute published in *The Saturday Review of Literature*, the President of Olivet College described his late faculty member and what that residency entailed:

Specific lectures, endless discussions, yes. Countless hours working on manuscripts with students and aspiring writers

from all over the section, yes. But it was more just his presence amongst us and what he stood for, his passion for the
"humaner letters," his insistence that quality and integrity,
such as the true artist lives by, are the only things that count
in civilization, his relish of life, his capacity for enjoyment of
the *menus plaisirs,* his amazing self-discipline for work despite a contrary appearance of indolence . . . and above all
his indefatigable and spendthrift giving of himself to all who
sincerely came to him for advice and help, both human and
artistic. These are the things that impressed themselves
upon the life of the College and upon all who came into
close contact with him.[19]

And so I imagine Ford Madox Ford, early to work in the
dark of the day, taking his place in the overstuffed chair in
the ill-lit library basement, rereading Horace or Hazlitt or
Hawthorne, making his case pro or measured or con, speaking his writing, each pause an ellipsis, at preoccupied Janice
or dutiful Jack. Then halfway through his self-imposed allocation of a thousand words per session he emerges from his
page-strewn warren and, in the presence of rapt though not
always or without exception enraptured students, commences his preprandial constitutional . . . a stroll across the
campus green, a measured professorial progress with pauses
in the consequence, both carpenter and walrus who spoke of
many things. There would be wind. There would be oak
leaves laureling him. There would be the prospect of cheese:
Brie, a good Stilton perhaps.

It's late autumn now, and exile has rendered our bard elegiac, recollecting his great predecessors in exile down the
years. Or should we perhaps more properly describe him as
full of a sort of anticipatory nostalgia for this sojourn he
foresees must end where he has labored unencumbered by
the press of public enterprise (those statesmen and ministers
and acknowledged legislators of the world whose attention
he once attempted to claim, whose company he claimed to
keep)? But this is purer, is it not, this high wine of artistic

commerce with the chatty shade of Villon by his side and the heady elixir of remembrance: *où sont les neiges d'antan?*

It snows in Michigan, it does; this wind has ice in its teeth. He shivers; his knee and arm ache. The boy with the notebook is attentive, ready to harvest what wisdom he sows; Ford rouses himself to make sense of the weather . . . "and the prophecy of a great darkness that has since descended on the minds of the world. For, indeed, Conrad might have claimed, like Flaubert, that if humanity had really read *Heart of Darkness* we might very well have been spared the horrors of our mondial debacle."[20]

By which the writer means, of course, the Great and previous War. But the storm clouds have been gathering, the storm troopers perfecting their lockstep and strut, and his shambling negotiation of a college green is merely a single man's walk. The March of Literature haply continues, but this its aging soldier is footsore and, it must be admitted, sore-hearted; what his old friend Joyce calls "syphilization" is gaining an ascendancy, and soon enough Herr Hitler will launch his foul campaign. Years before, in *No More Parades,* he had written: "Getting cattle into condition for the slaughterhouse. . . . They were as eager as bullocks running down by Camden Town to Smithfield Market. . . . Seventy percent of them would never come back. . . . But it's better to go to heaven with your skin shining and master of your limbs than as a hulking lout. . . . The Almighty's orderly room will welcome you better in all probability."[21]

Therefore, back to the march and the orderly room. Back after an inadequate lunch (midwestern ham, the alien corn, a cider that's to proper cider as the pea to pearl), then lumbering down to the library carrel and on to the Enlightenment, that bad joke we've played on ourselves. Back to the foredoomed enterprise of urging a new readership to read the actual lasting books, to open by implication possibly two or three of his previous own, to wave at Miss Amelia Earhart there in her garden (snipping chrysanthemums, deadheading peonies, a bright-eyed lady who lives in Olivet these years and also dreams of flight). Back through the stacks to his high-heaped desk and the borrowing and lending that constitute component parts of the one worthwhile activity, the clashing, jangling sounds words make, the way they can conjure the sky of Provence or a cottage by the shingle via language, only language, the deep draught of Château d'Yquem imagined with its liquid lambent consolation: taste and aftertaste.

He read and wrote and read. He wrote and read and wrote. As his creature Tietjens says, "But the thing is to be able to stick to the integrity of your character, whatever earthquake sets the house tumbling over your head."[22] He stuck to it; he cleaved to his last to the last. And sometimes in a quiet house, when staring at the bookshelves' sag or breathing that particular must attaching to a sea-thumbed page, I *see* Ford Madox Ford, I *hear* him, though I never saw or heard him while alive. We can be haunted, can't we, by ghosts who wheeze through carious teeth that literature is marching, marching, and there's a Republic of Letters whose tattered brilliant banner an old man mad about writing furls and hoists and waves. . . .

Anywhere Out of the World

Travel writing is, I think, coeval with writing itself. We move and remember the place that we left; from a distance we send letters home. Those scribes who first kept laundry lists in Nineveh or Babylon, those men in Egypt naming names belong to the one genre. An account of journeys taken or a report at journey's end, a message from the provinces or dispatch from the capital: each must be written down. The Tibetan Book of the Dead, the Hindu epic *Mahabarata*, *The Tale of Genji* on his wanderings: all these record departure and new terrain traversed. And there's retentiveness also entailed; when the bear goes over the mountain to see what he can see, he carries with him—if he be a writer—a computer or quill pen.

In the western tradition of literature, the common denominator of *The Odyssey* and *Pilgrim's Progress*, *The Canterbury Tales* and *The Divine Comedy*—not to mention *Don Quixote* or *Moby-Dick* or *Faust*—is near-constant motion. One way to read the Book of Genesis is to consider that expulsion as a journey out of Eden; the long travail of Moses is a hunt for promised land. So too is *The Aeneid* a travelogue that starts in Troy and ends hard years later in Rome. "The Wanderer" and "The Seafarer" are descriptions of water-logged distance traversed; Captain Cook and Magellan and Lewis and Clark get parsed now for their prose. Although we're not certain how widely he traveled, Avon's Bard set many of his plays abroad; it sometimes seems as though *all* texts we hold to be enduring ones evoke a world of wonders that at first seem passing strange. . . .

This holds just as true for those who—like Jane Austen or Emily Dickinson—remain inside the house. Imagination need be neither time- nor space-bound, finally, and writing gets done at the desk. The stay-at-home may take projected trips or may, like Marcel Proust, remember where he lived when young; *À la Recherche du Temps Perdu* is a remembrance not merely of time but scenes and places past. The writer may be imprisoned, as was the Oscar Wilde of *De Profundis,* or, like Charles Darwin, confined to a cabin on the H.M.S. *Beagle*—but each and all of them are travel writers in the largest sense: I have *been* there, *witnessed* it, and am come alone to tell thee what I saw. . . .

Marco Polo—who may or may not have gone where he said—announced his voyage thus:

> Emperors and kings, dukes and marquises, counts, knights, and townsfolk, and all will find all the great wonders and curiosities of Greater Armenia and Persia, of the Tartars and of India, and of many other territories. Our book will relate them to you plainly in due order, as they were related by Messer Marco Polo, a wise and noble citizen of Venice, who has seen them with his own eyes. There is also much here that he has not seen but has heard from men of credit and veracity. . . .[1]

Those who once were travelers are tourists now; those who embark for points unknown, whether pilgrims or Crusaders, have been supplanted by the gang who follow where a tour guide leads. Open any airline magazine or travel section in the Sunday paper and you'll find an industry devoted to what Mark Twain called *Innocents Abroad*. To begin with it was only the nobility, or their cast-off sons and marriageable daughters, who went away for pleasure or profit; in the last two hundred years all that has changed. As John Julius Norwich puts it, in his anthology, *A Taste for Travel:*

> By 1815 . . . travel had ceased to be the prerogative of the gentry; the roads of the Continent were now thronged with middle-class Englishmen who had made their fortunes in the first wave of the Industrial Revolution and were anxious to show that they too could understand and appreciate all that Europe had to offer. Increased numbers soon resulted in improved facilities: the first cross-Channel steamer was introduced in 1816, a regular service between Dover and Calais was inaugurated in 1821 and five years later there were almost as many crossings as there are today. In France and Germany, Italy and Switzerland, hotels sprang up like mushrooms along the main routes.[2]

Today it's easy to forget how recent was the shift. Those fabled early travelers who set out from Baghdad or Beijing or Calcutta may well have done so with servants, but their exploits are reported as individual: X made ten thousand miles on foot, Y traveled twenty years and through forty kingdoms, Z acquired fifty languages and a hundred children before he came back home. *A Sentimental Journey Through France and Italy*, as Laurence Sterne would have it, was one man's ambling ramble. The romantics on their walking tours of Switzerland or the Lake District wandered with a boon companion or, more often than not, alone. Lord Norwich turns up his well-bred English nose at the idea of collective travel and those who pay with vouchers for a prearranged forced march:

> The man who started the rot, I fear, was that disagreeable old abstainer Thomas Cook, who, already by the middle of the century, had developed the idea of insulating his clients

as far as possible from the uncouth conditions all too frequently prevailing in foreign parts by swathing them in a protective cocoon of block bookings, meal vouchers and—most dangerous of all—temperance. He began indeed by offering them even more: on the very first excursion that he ever organized, which took place on Monday 5 July, 1841, the 570 people intrepid enough to venture—at the cost of one shilling—the ten miles from Leicester to Loughsborough and back enjoyed the services of a full brass band, to say nothing of tea and buns at Mr. Paget's Park. The age of the tourist had arrived.[3]

Most contemporary travel writers set out with the more or less conscious purpose of writing it all down. The death of Wilfrid Thesiger rings a kind of death knell also for the solitary wanderer whose trip is open-ended, with no planned return. Paul Theroux and Jonathan Raban, I'd guess, go nowhere nowadays without a contract and a camera; when Gretel Erhlich or Terry Tempest Williams heads off into the wilderness, it's with the apparatus of retention and the likely prospect of turning their trip into text. Where once there was just Baedecker or a *Guide Bleu*, we now have whole travel sections in any self-respecting bookstore; there's nearly nowhere on the globe that hasn't had its witness and been in purple prose or Technicolor described. . . .

The last four names I've named (Theroux, Raban, Erhlich, Willliams) are working today, and it's not an accident that two of them are women. This was not always the case. For reasons too obvious to belabor, the travel writers of the fifteenth or the eighteenth century were almost without exception male, and most of them well-educated and well-heeled. Several of the true heroes of the genre are its early heroines: Mary Kingsley and Freya Stark went where almost literally no single woman had gone before, and Beryl Markham and Martha Gellhorn are easily the adventuring equals of Antoine de Saint-Exupéry and Ernest Hemingway. One way of looking at the issue of "women's liberation" would be to do a statistical analysis of just such reportage;

there are more women writing for publication now than at any previous moment in our history. Travel writing is a genre that's no longer gender-bound. . . .

> For my part, I travel not to go anywhere, but to go. I travel
> for travel's sake. The great affair is to move.
>   Robert Louis Stevenson, *Travels with a Donkey*

Within such overarching inclusiveness, there are distinctions to draw. Books about Julius Caesar or Abraham Lincoln or Joan of Arc are travel writing in the largest sense, but their focused exploration has to do with the world of the past. Adventure tales through time and space aren't within my compass here: historical novels or escapist fantasy—from *A Connecticut Yankee in King Arthur's Court* to *Canopus in Argos*—are travel books imagined, not reported on. So equally with *1984* or *2001*, which once seemed future-facing, or *20,000 Leagues Under the Sea* and the whole field of science fiction: books about robots and extraterrestrials are travel writing of a kind, but not the kind I mean.

A ship's log makes an inadvertent book, as do a naturalist's field notes: the journal of a journey with no prior thought of audience. Much of what we read today is a by-blow of such voyaging: the first account of the North Pole, the first of North America, were composed by authors who would not describe themselves primarily as such and whose "letters home" were not dispatched with publication in mind. That suggestively named professional, the "underwriter," might require details, and the owners of a galleon would make "manifest" the lists of crew and cargo, but personal opinion is what we as readers hunger for; it invigorates eyewitnessing and quickens the long-dead.

There's a subset of the genre from, as it were, the captive class: a slave's or bondswoman's narrative, a farmer's wife carried off by an Indian tribe. Not every traveler is literate or maintains a journal; not every Robinson Crusoe finds pen and paper to hand. But think of Mungo Park or Richard Burton, John Speke or Henry Stanley—those wanderers who made their fortune by reporting news of Africa—and *intention* enters in. When Boswell followed Dr Johnson on his journey through the Hebrides, he knew he would remember it and come back with a book. . . .

> Travel, in the younger sort, is a part of education; in the elder, a part of experience. He that travelleth into a country before he hath some entrance into the language, goeth to school, and not to travel.   Francis Bacon, *Of Travel*

Two strands seem worth disentangling in this common cloth. First, and perhaps most frequent, is a report from far away—the news sent back from a little known or rarely visited part of the world: a tribe or terrain that appears inhospitable, a record of hardships endured. The writer travels long and hard and stares wide-eyed at landscape and behavior that feels foreign. The place and the people merit describing, and though we no longer report on three-headed men and single-breasted women—or fire-breathing dragons, Loch Ness monsters, and the like—such travelogues traffic in distance, the wonder of what's hard to find.

Almost by definition, this variety of travel writing depends on the first view. The voyager attains a premised end and does so *once*—or, possibly, buoyed by success and fame, not to mention an expense account, returns. The point is, however, that he or she goes as a stranger, and what's remarkable in these accounts depends on first impressions: a freshness, an alertness, a sense of something *new*. So it isn't deep-rooted knowledge but an amateur's enthusiasm that signals destination and establishes the tone. A great enough artist may perhaps be able to convey such alertness during a visit to London or Rome, but the odds are better if the place attained is Patagonia or Uttar Pradesh.

This sort of exploration is wide-eyed and improvisational; it reports on happy accident or unhappy being blown off course, and the writer profits from prior ignorance. Indeed, it's almost a *sine qua non* of the genre; you can't undertake a voyage to map your own hometown. So expertise means not familiarity but a fresh encounter with the alien, the other. Travel writing of this kind requires a physical distance—the wanderer on train or steamship or horseback or dogsled, going somewhere hard to get to, and for the first time. Whatever he or she reports is more than what was known before or what we as readers knew. Discovery is crucial here: the difficult journey "anywhere out of the world."

The phrase is Baudelaire's. He meant by this a yearning for what's far away, not familiar and a cause for spleen; the bazaar and "bizarre" are cognate terms, and the lure of the tropics or a pure uncharted ice floe is, for the heartsore, strong. Such stories start, often as not, in the city, with a man or woman sick of worldliness or with a "damp, drizzly November in my soul"—as Melville's Ishmael puts it—and in thrall to the unknown. It's surely not an accident that Melville's major commercial success was as a travel writer; his books *Typee* and *Omoo* retail exotica. This is the sort of book in which the voyager hears siren songs and wanders where they beckon; it deals with the South Seas or the hidden mountain kingdom of Nepal. Again—almost by definition—the trip is undertaken alone. And the farther the better, the farthest the best: nothing difficult is easy and few rainbows end next door. . . .

In the twenty-first century, however, such destinations grow harder to find, and solitary explorations are a thing of the vanishing past. When the first westerner made his disguised way into Mecca or her camel-assisted trek across the Sahara, he or she could not have imagined the legions being herded down those well-worn paths today. Sir Walter Raleigh and Hakluyt shared as voyagers a breath-held sense of danger, an implicit and sometimes explicit assertion that much was at stake and at risk. War correspondents belong within this category, though the purpose of their travel is not to chart terrain. And the governing verb form is an imperative: reader, look over my shoulder. Spend two years with me before the mast or follow where the song lines lead; few have come this way before. . . .

Much of the commercial popularity of *Seven Pillars of Wisdom* or the novel *Lost Horizon*—to take only a pair of examples of stories retrieved from the "ends of the earth"—derived from just such a remoteness. But now that the globe is a village, it's nowhere near as difficult to reach the gulf of Aqaba or the town of Kathmandu, and reports from what used to be called Arabia or the Orient require not a rare first view but grounded expertise. Books about smoke jumpers and coal miners and bridge builders are in this sense travel writing; they provide the reader with detailed information about a way of life and set of skills unlike his or her own. There's a special subset of the genre recovered from those who failed to return: the letters gathered from a battlefield or found in a tent in arctic tundra or raised up from the sea. So now we get *The Perfect Storm* and *Into Thin Air*—accounts of a kind of extremity; the action itself may be special and strange, but the landscape has been long since mapped. . . .

Here's the whole of chapter XVII, "Concerning Owls," from *The Natural History of Iceland*, written by Niels Horrebow in 1758: "There are no owls of any kind in the whole island."

By contrast, therefore, are contemporary books that deal with semipermanence in a "New Found Land." This is the sort of account—think of Peter Mayle or Francis Mayes—where the stranger settles down and reports on what it meant to grow acclimatized to Provence or Tuscany. Here the narrative arc almost always consists of ignorance that yields to understanding, a bedazzled attraction to a place that deepens into love. And it requires the clarification provided by hindsight and time. The writer reports on local custom and how he or she—first quizzical and then convinced—learns how the natives cook or farm or court or kill or renovate a house. Often these dispatches too are sent back from "the field"; more often they are written after the fact, as memoir.

This variety of book is less about wandering than sitting still, but it too belongs to the genre. It is powered by the elegiac impulse rather more than by astonishment; it reports on custom embraced rather than in shock recorded, and the pattern is one of incremental pleasure as the writer settles in. There's a standard shift of attitude; what at first seemed nonsensical starts to make sense; what required explaining to start with grows, over time, self-evident. It's the relativist's credo, in effect: "When in Rome, do as the Romans do."

Here it matters if the writer arrives in "Rome" as an adult or was to the manner if not manor born. If the former—as with Mayle and Mayes—the book may be written while still in residence; if the latter, the perspective shifts and Arcady's at a remove. "I *had* a farm in Africa" (Isak Dinesen's famous phrase) is the operational mode—the pluperfect tense suggesting it's all over but the writing; memory preserves a place and time long gone.

While the first of our two modes consists of a report from afar, this second one, by contrast, speaks of lost familiarity. The witness has moved on. From the distance of both space and time, the writer reconstructs his youth as a tenant farmer's son in the South, the rigors of her childhood in Botswana or Bengal. The beloved mother or grandfather is dead, the custom of sheep-shearing or snake charming has been altered by the trappings of modernity. The tribe that once was unencumbered now watches TV through the cold winter nights, the shaman owns a cell phone, and what used to be unending prairie is now a housing tract. If the writer writes of vanished youth, he or she may do so for the purpose of score settling or as a lament for yesteryear or with a dry-eyed dispassion; what's constant is this sense of distance and a world elsewhere. . . .

It's the difference, in effect, between an act of *discovery* and one of *recovery*; as an autobiographical account, the writer reports on information gained or innocence long lost. Therefore the noun of travel depends upon its yoked preposition; it's travel *to* or travel *from,* and much is entailed by the shift.

Here's a line of cultural anthropology from one of the first tourists, Herodotus: "Apart from the fact that they prostitute their daughters, the Lydian way of life is not unlike our own."

Consider, by contrast, this account by an outraged Englishman, one Dr. Birch, of his time in the presence of Peter the Great (who founded St. Petersburg in 1703) and how the Tsar entertained.

> There are twenty-four cooks belonging to the kitchen of the Russian court, who are all Russians; and, as people of that nation use a great deal of onions, garlic, and train oyl, in dressing their meat, and employ linseed and walnut oyl for their provisions, there is such an intolerable stink in their kitchen, that no stranger is able to bear it, especially the cooks being such nasty fellows that the very sight of them is enough to turn one's stomach. . . .
>
> The number of the persons invited is commonly two or three hundred, though there is room for no more than about an hundred, at four or five tables. But as there is no place assigned to any body, and none of the Russians are willing to go home with an empty stomach, every body is obliged to seize his chair and hold it with all his force, if he will not have it snatched from him.
>
> The Czar being come in, and having chosen a place for himself, there is such scuffling and fighting for chairs, that nothing more scandalous can be seen in any country. . . .
>
> At great entertainments it frequently happens that nobody is allowed to go out of the room from noon till midnight. Hence it is easy to imagine what pickle a room must

be in, that is full of people who drink like beasts, and none
of them escape being dead drunk.

They often tie eight or ten young mice on a string, and
hide them under green peas, or in such soups as the Russians have the greatest appetites to; which sets them a *kecking* and vomiting in a most beastly manner, when they
come to the like in their pastries, and when the company
have eat them up, they tell them what stuff they have in
their guts.[4]

Let me confess to personal experience of the several kinds of
travel writing I've described. Some fifteen years ago or so, I
had a friend—a publisher—who wanted to revive the genre,
or at least to make a commercial venture in America of what
was popular abroad. His notion had been to commission
books by "an interesting mind in an interesting place," and
he flatteringly invited me to be one of his first authors in
what became the "Traveler" series of Atlantic Monthly
Press. He was well funded, well disposed, and at the lunch
where we discussed the project I had too many Bloody
Marys and my head, it must be admitted, was a good deal less
than clear.

So was his. I remember asking if he'd pay for a trip up
Everest and he said, Sure, Sherpas, the whole show. . . . I remember asking if he'd pay for outriders in the Outback and
he said, The entire rig, why not? . . . So by the time lunch
was over and we'd gone our separate ways I had effectively
signed up, signed on; and soon enough a contract arrived,
saying simply "Nicholas Delbanco, Travel Book." But I had
no idea at all of where to travel to.

Reality set in. In sober truth, I felt too old and unadven-
turous for the Himalayas or Australia's barren interior; my
wife and I had two daughters by then, and I was happily domestic and didn't want to leave for long or travel far away.
The more I thought about it, the less I was inclined to try for
category one of what I've been trying to categorize, and so
fell back on the notion of category two. This required a land-

scape of which I'd had a more or less sustained experience: a report, in effect, on strangeness grown familiar. The place I settled on was one I'd often settled in, and it did qualify as a beloved countryside: Provence. In time it did become a book: *Running in Place: Scenes from the South of France.*

But the problem, of course, was that Provence has been described often and well; it has been charted to the millimeter, and one can barely visit a museum or café without encountering a legion of other travel writers taking notes. It's scarcely *terra incognita*, and there's the real risk of cliché. My solution, such as it was, was to turn inward—and to report upon the way the landscape looked to me in childhood, young manhood, young married manhood, as a father of a daughter, then two daughters. It was an inward trip at least as much as an outer exploration, and for me at least the journey proved rewarding.

It's difficult to know, in this epoch of Heisenberg and Einstein, what is absolute, what relative, and why. Do we change as witnesses or does what we witness change, or both? Does it alter because of the viewing, and is our estimate altered by the very consciousness of sight? These issues of philosophy and science are domestic riddles also; was it *always* just like this, and did we fail to notice? So the chance to see for a second or third time a place we remember vividly is a chance worth taking; the six or seven stays in Provence on which *Running in Place* reports were, in effect, stages of age. . . .

As a result of that book—it appeared in 1989 and has been reprinted since—I acquired some small reputation as a travel writer. This was an unintended consequence, and one I had my doubts about, but the phone did ring. Soon I found myself becoming precisely the sort of voyager I disparaged above: the one with an expense account who goes not so much to blaze a trail as to make certain it will be well marked. So I wrote a piece for *Travel and Leisure* called "Up in the U.P." because I'd never been to that part of Michigan and needed an excuse to go; for much the same reason and because they waived the entrance fee, I wrote on Greenfield

Village and the Henry Ford Museum. The Greek government, to take a more romantic example, wanted to establish
the Mani peninsula as a tourist destination, and my wife and
I bounced and jiggled along the new-paved roads of the region in order to rate hotels. It's a wonderful part of the Pelo-
ponnesus and I have no regrets; a glossy travel magazine
footed the bill, and when Olympic Airways lost track of Elena's suitcase, they bestirred themselves mightily to find it
once I dropped that magazine's name.

But it's a strânge way to see a landscape—spurious, largely, and traversed with the subsidized intention of spending a
good deal of money in order to encourage your readership to
do the same; that original impulse to escape has been transformed past recognition in the travel pages of *House & Garden* and *Gourmet*. It's a far cry indeed from *Mornings in Mexico*, D. H. Lawrence's travel memoir, or Eric Newby's
classic *A Short Walk in the Hindu Kush*.

I name this last because decades ago we too passed
through the Hindu Kush from Kabul to Jalalabad. Elena and
I hired a driver to pilot us along the lunar landscape; this was
well before the Taliban controlled the countryside, but even
so it seemed threatful and fierce: steep-pitched gorges,
boulder-strewn hills, no water one could see. It's hard to
conceive how this might have been the Silk Road or a populous trade route, since nothing in it represents prosperity or
seems to welcome and enable life.

We set out in the early morning and left paved roads behind. There were endless-seeming vistas of dried mud and
dun-colored chasms, the track a slightly flatter, slightly pur-
posive declivity through the surrounding wastes. At a certain
point we stopped for lunch—wax paper–wrapped sandwiches the hotel in Kabul had provided—and because there was,
the driver said, a bit of both water and shade.

All I could see was rock. We parked in the flat sheltered
space and stepped out to stretch. The wind was high. I
steeled myself and took a very short walk in the Hindu Kush
and then the wind shifted so with total clarity I heard, "Do
you take lemon or sugar—one or two lumps? And do you

prefer milk or cream in your tea?" It was, it turned out, the wife of the British ambassador, and she was regaling some visitor of consequence with cucumber sandwiches and a proper British refreshment while the chauffeur dusted off the Jag; this dry oasis was the recognized stopping place on the road to Jalalabad, and there were two cars parked on the two sides of the one rock. One has to travel long and far to be alone. . . .

I have travelled a good deal in Concord.
Henry David Thoreau, *Walden, I*

Charles Baudelaire, twenty years old, was sent from France to India in 1841. Like many of the great French rebel artists, he had been raised in propriety; his stepfather was a general, an ambassador, and, finally, a senator. That worthy and the poet's mother hoped their young man might become a lawyer; he was supposed to be weaned from wanton ways— though he had contracted, already, the syphilis that would destroy him—and go abroad for two years. He was to leave behind his dissolute life, his taste for prostitutes and unpaid bills and the lure of drink and drugs.

But "Anywhere out of the world" for Baudelaire proved an inner destination; his travels were truncated and few. When the boat put into Mauritius for repairs, the poet insisted on turning around; he reversed the voyage out. Was it an access of boredom, fear, homesickness? Was it, perhaps, a sense that his vocation called so strongly that he need not roam? It was on this journey that he composed the first of the *Fleurs du Mal*. At any rate, the yearning thirst to "sail away" (the title of a song by the far better-traveled Noel Coward) seems to have been rapidly slaked. World-weariness for Coward would be a condition to relish and, in the relishing, put to good use; *ennui* for Baudelaire would be not the exception but rule.

Once safely back in Paris, and having attained his majori-ty, the poet squandered his inheritance with an adept's fervor; living the life of a dandy in the Hotel Lauzun on the Ile Saint-Louis, he met Jeanne Duval and—not necessarily in this order—made the acquaintance of Courbet and Delacroix and began his translations of Poe. The long slow decline from *luxe, calme et volupté* to debt and degradation proved ever more rapid and steep, a journey he could not reverse.

We have the great photograph from 1863. Baudelaire stares balefully out at the camera of Étienne Carjat, dark eyes half shadowed beneath the white brow. We have Manet's engraving of the same face and a lithograph by Rouault. Rouault made a series of *portraits intimes,* though what he renders here is the portrait by Carjat. Rodin too tried his hand at the head—though far less often and less daringly than with the head of Balzac. In each version of the poet's face there is the same rife blankness, the high dome and the lick of hair and lack of *bonhomie;* things *matter,* Baudelaire seems to be saying, and I refuse to smile. He died in 1867, with much of his writing unpublished and all of his works out of print.

The "advice to travelers" component of the literature is a category in itself. Here's a series of non sequiturs from a Russian primer: *Hossfield's New Practical Method for Learning the Russian Language,* 1903:

> What did Susanna reply?
>   Susanna made no reply, but Eleonora Karpova suddenly approached and said that Susanna liked music very much and played on the piano most beautifully.
>   Then Mr. Ratch must have married a widow the first time?

If art's high charge is to "make it new," the novelty itself may prove germane. A reader, after all, encounters Place A or Character B for the first time on a first page, and has no previous knowledge of that countryside or face. The scribe de*scribes* it; we plot the coordinates of imagined terrain, then act as its surveyor, and sometimes this seems simpler when the landscape as such is not long established or known. I mean by this that wide-eyed witnessing is as feasible—*more* so, perhaps—if what we witness is new to us too. A tourist's first visit to Beijing will yield a different impression than a fifth or fifteenth. To be "silent on a peak in Darien" is a function of "*First* Looking into Chapman's Homer," and Keats was bedazzled by the vista in a way the classics scholar cannot replicate. Repeated exposure supplies expertise, but it's the amateur's excitement we hunt for in a book.

The armchair traveler in this regard becomes the necessary secret sharer of the travel writer. The act of exploration that the best books offer is mirrored by the forward march we make with each turned page. When you travel you take yourself with you, and adventure happens in a hammock as well as on a storm-tossed, hand-constructed raft. The conscious voyager—whether solo or part of a party, whether hired or on some private quest, whether male or female, young or old—is almost always hunting change, in search of something new.

It may be as literal as discovery: a stretch of coast not mapped before, a mountain range not previously climbed or named. More likely nowadays it's an inward-bound journey, and the writer reports on distance traversed by the wandering self. Almost by definition (again I exclude those accounts of arctic expeditions found beside the frozen body or those ship's logs retrieved from a drowned sailor's sea chest), to record a voyage is to return enlarged. When the bear went over the mountain, he found another mountain—or at least had a story to tell.

Letter from Namibia

It is a long journey—two nights and a day by plane. My routing was Detroit due east to Amsterdam, then Amsterdam south to Johannesburg, then northwest once again to Windhoek, the capital of Namibia. An empty, ancient landscape surrounds that "windy corner"; a mile beyond the Windhoek International Airport, all is parched grass and dust-whitened shrubs.

The Alps are 200 million years old, the mountains of the Sperrgebiet 900 million and counting. Wind and erosion have worn them down; what's left is wrinkled, stooped. The feel of age is palpable here; the two-leafed plant *Welwitschia mirabilis* can live a thousand years. The cave paintings of Altamira and Lascaux were produced in—these figures are approximate—10,000 B.C.; some date the art on Brandberg mountain as 30,000 years old. In such a dry unchangingness, it's difficult to know.

"When I grow up I shall go there," wrote Joseph Conrad about "the heart of darkness"; his Congo is well mapped by now, and far more populous. Three quarters of the population of Namibia (a nation of less than two million) live in the far north of the country and on comparatively fertile ground. I did not travel to Ovamboland, where the rivers always run, and for the first ten days of driving saw no traffic lights.

"God must have been angry when he made this place"—so goes the Bushman saying. The expression endures though the speakers have changed; Bushmen today construe that sobriquet an insult and now are called the Khoi-San. The iconic "Mama Sarah"—a Bushman woman displayed as a curiosity in Europe when she arrived there in 1810—has been repatriated after "exile" and her bones buried with pomp. In Europe she descended into poverty and prostitution, but President Thabo Mbeki of South Africa eulogized her in a memorial service celebrating her casket's return. "Sarah Bartmann should never have been transported to Europe. Sarah Bartmann should never have been robbed of her name. . . . Sarah Bartmann should never have been stripped of her Khoi-San and African identity and paraded in Europe as a savage monstrosity. . . . It was not the abused human being who was monstrous, but those who abused her."[1]

On the second day of flying, I had a layover in Amsterdam—long enough to leave the airport and travel into town. I wanted to visit the Rijksmuseum and the collection there. It had been years since I'd seen that national treasure, the Cranachs and Cuyps and Ruisdaels and paintings by Rubens and Hals. As its artists indicate, their time was a period of expansion for the Dutch Republic, with its ship-crowded harbors and cloud-studded skies. The most celebrated canvas in the Rijksmuseum—Rembrandt's *The Night Watch*—shows prosperity on a large scale. The faces portrayed here are plump yet severe, the lace at their wrists finely spun. Nothing is impossible, these commercial folk seem to be saying, no reach beyond our grasp. . . .

The picture I studied, however, was small: *Woman Reading a Letter*, by Johannes Vermeer. That artist lived from 1632 to 1675; the first settlement on Capetown—established by the Dutch East India Company as a supply station for those who sailed around the Cape—came at the start of his painting career, in 1652. There would have been no Windhoek yet, no hardy *voortrekkers* gone north. Yet much of

Vermeer's work juxtaposes an interior and domestic world to that of exploration; this woman holding a letter stands before a map.

What is she reading; who wrote to her; why? Her emotions are vivid yet veiled. It's clear the letter matters, matters to her passionately; she has raised it to her breast and clasps it with both hands. She may in fact be pregnant; her stomach gently swells. But does the folded page announce her beloved's intention to visit next month? Does it inform her he's dead, or delayed, or having a wonderful time in the Indies and wishing she were there? Is it from her husband she receives news, or her father, her sister or child? Are the tidings conveyed good or bad? Does she read for the first time or fifth?

On the room's wall hangs a fabric map of which we're shown perhaps a quarter; it's vast. There are suggestions of mountains, of oceans and coasts; the colors replicate the colors of her skirt. Vermeer's subject offers her profile; the map casts a shadow; the source of the light is off canvas, up left. What this beautiful woman is reading has caused her to rise from her seat at table; the chair has been pushed back. There may well be somebody else in the room, though not within the area of the visible composition: a servant or painter watching her read, as do we. Hers is a solitude breached. But whatever the news and whatever her mood, it's manifest this woman pays *attention*, a rapt and close-hauled scrutiny of a world elsewhere brought home.

Namibia was named as such and constituted as a nation only a dozen years ago. Portuguese navigators, seeking the sea route to the Indies, began charting the Atlantic coastline in the late fifteenth century, dropping anchor at Cape Cross, Walvis Bay, and Dias Point. Then, for more than three hundred years, the nation-states of Europe left the inland expanse alone. A few explorers, prospectors, and evangelicals made their way through, but "Southwest" proved uninviting and its climate harsh. Jacobus Coetse crossed the Orange

River in 1760; he was followed by explorers such as Hendrik Hop and Pieter Brand. In 1793 Pieter Pienaar anchored in Walvis Bay; Heinrich Schmelen founded a German evangelical mission in 1815. But not until the discovery of diamonds did the place seem a commercial prize worth having, and even then its settlement was desultory. The English annexed Walvis Bay but did not enlarge their influence; the German trader Adolf Lüderitz petitioned the German leadership for protection of the town to which he gave his name in 1884. Chancellor Otto von Bismarck agreed.

This most recently independent of the African countries belonged to the German empire until World War I. It was the first German possession to fall to the Allies; a capitulation ceremony took place in Windhoek's Rathaus in 1915. After the Treaty of Versailles the territory was entrusted to the Union of South Africa as a "c" mandate; this agreement, signed in Geneva, gave the union power to administer the former colony, though with the understanding that self-government would at some point ensue. However, that understanding proved notional, and South Africa retained control of the territory's wealth.

Resistance grew. SWAPO—the South West African People's Organization—began as a nonviolent pressure group in 1960; by the middle of that decade, however, its cadres were receiving guerrilla training in Egypt, and on August 26, 1966—now known as "Namibia Day"—insurgents fought with security forces at Omgulumubashe. Throughout the 1970s and '80s, SWAPO waged war for independence, making of the countryside and cityscape armed camps. Arson and theft and cattle slaughter and assassination were not the exception but rule. Barbed concertina wire still guerdons private property, and fortified watchtowers rise from the center of farms.

After decades of such insurgency, South Africa had had enough and withdrew from its protectorship. At midnight on March 20, 1990, at a ceremony in Windhoek, the South African flag was lowered and replaced by the newly designed flag of the Republic of Namibia. Because of its valuable minerals (a diamond zone is cordoned off) and its small population, Namibia is now comparatively wealthy. The scourge of AIDS is omnipresent, although—at least by contrast with neighboring Botswana—not yet widely visible; public works proceed apace. The Wambo and Kavango and the Nama and Herero and Damara peoples are at present peace. Their wars were fierce; they may resume—but as of this writing the country seems more stable than South Africa across its southern border, Angola to its north.

In February 1990, Shafishuna Samuel Najoma was unanimously elected president by members of the constituent assembly; he remains in office today. A storied hero of resistance, he stands in much the same relation to his country as did Kwame Nkrumah of Ghana or Jomo Kenyatta of Kenya; a member of the dominant Owambo tribe, he was born in 1929 and is no longer young. Benignly smiling down from portraits hung on government buildings and out from photos in newspapers, President "Sam" Nujoma has declared his intention not to run again and to preserve the constitution he himself composed; he has no obvious successor, however, and there are those who mutter that Robert Mugabe of Zimbabwe once said much the same. Whether Nujoma will retain as a model the example of Nelson Mandela—who did indeed retire—or follow where Mugabe led, it is too soon to say.[2]

In my young manhood I traveled a lot, and often to countries it's no longer simple to see. I visited Iran and Afghanistan, for example, and have witnessed firefights in Sri Lanka and Colombia and Greece. Displacement seemed almost an end in itself, and a much-stamped passport somehow a form of achievement; *A Long Desire*—as Evan Connell Jr. tellingly titles his book about such wanderers—kept me on the move.

Of late, however, that thirst had been slaked and wanderlust reined in. My roads are paved, well-traveled ones, and my destinations capital cities, a middle-aged man in hotels. So there was something doubly welcome about the list of flight announcements posted on the Johannesburg Airport departure board. Here was the old familiar sense of strange-ness, the sight of men and women dressed in what appeared to be costumes and eating food I couldn't recognize and speaking languages I couldn't understand. That early morn-ing—and I had been to none of them—the destinations read:

Windhoek: 9:00
Victoria Falls: 9:15
Luanda: 9:15
Mauritius: 9:15
Maputo: 9:30
Gabarone (via Nairobi): 9:45
Marozini: 9:55
Lusaka: 10:00
Maun: 10:00

My companions were my Ann Arbor neighbor, George K., whose wife Danielle awaited us in Windhoek, and a friend of theirs, Patti H. A South African cardiologist, Eddie G., and the Ks' two sons—Andrew, sixteen, and James, eighteen—completed our party: seven in all. Danielle met us at the airport; we piled into a van. She herself had been born in South Africa, and her grandfather was buried on "Erichs-felde," the property north of the town of Okahandja he bought in 1938 and lived on, developed, and loved. A Ger-man industrialist, old Erich—whose photograph still hangs on the wall and whose grave is on the farm—worked for the diamond cartel, De Beers, and established railways and man-aged to stay clear of Hitler's malevolent leveling rage; of thirty-seven business leaders invited to a meeting with *der Führer*, he alone declined to attend and he alone survived.

"Erich's Fields" have been reduced since his death and parceled and sold off—but there are still some 13,000 hectares, or more than 30,000 acres, remaining. The new generation is far-flung and some of them can visit only rarely; Danielle and George had not been there for years. There are issues of collective ownership and maintenance costs to defray and capital improvements to underwrite and political uncertainty for all. But while they still had access to Namibia I ought to come along, they said, and such an invitation is not easy to refuse. Although the prospect of an organized commercial "safari" holds neither charm nor interest for me, the chance to see a country from its back roads and a camp tent was not to be missed. I bought a ticket and malaria pills and refurbished my old Olivetti portable typewriter and left.

If the globe's a jigsaw puzzle, it's clear that southwest Africa should edge up against southeast South America. The tectonic shift that tore those two apart and gave rise to the myth of Atlantis has marked this place indelibly; its beauty is desolate, sere. The Kalahari Desert has a game fence running north to south like a woven wire version of the Great Wall of China; this is supposed to keep dread foot-and-mouth disease at bay. Tall fences line the highway here, and crews were repairing the worn surface of the road; the land looked overhunted, overgrazed. We drove two hours north. There are police checkpoints at the outskirts of Windhoek and Okahandja, but the policemen sat in lounge chairs and waved us past. I asked what they were looking for, and George said, "Poachers, mostly." Now cattle and game are protected; what flourishes is goats.

Our driver was Erichsfelde's manager, Hörst A. He and his wife Renate and their two-year-old son Ralph would be leaving soon, he said, to return to Hörst's family's farm. His father had grown old and needed help. They were sorry to be moving on; they had enjoyed and were good at their work, but this was an obligation as well as a chance for ownership. In the meantime, everything was shipshape and they were attempting to replace themselves; there would be a series of interviews set up for prospective successors.

Renate is a botanist; she has written on "Bush encroachment in Namibia" and coauthored a position paper with the jaw-cracking title of "Long-Term Compositional Change of the Thornbush Savanna in Namibia: An Example from a Cattle Farm in Central Namibia." That farm is Erichsfelde, which, in 1963, sustained 1,300 head of cattle. Then foot-and-mouth disease broke out; the grass was drought-depleted and the bush encroached. Now 300 head are all it can sustain, and the farm has "diversified." This means that oryx and kudu and eland and springbok have been allowed to multiply until "harvested" by visiting hunters—men from Germany and elsewhere who pay handsomely for trophies shot under detailed procedures and with strict supervision. There are three taxidermists on the way to Windhoek Airport; the farm retains the meat.

Hörst is a smiling, stocky man, his wife intense and lean. He is taciturn, she voluble; between the two of them, says George, they lick the platter clean. They live in the "Manager's House" on the property; there are several smaller outbuildings, built of local brick and stucco, and we were allocated quarters among them: the adults in a three-room bungalow with patio and sitting room, the boys in a thatched-roof circular structure called a rondavel. I thanked Hörst for the ride.

"Pleasure," he said, and offered a three-stage handshake—the full palm, then the fingertips, then the palm again—that I would learn to expect. "Pleasure" means "You're welcome" or "Don't mention it" as well as "Good to see you"; it's a multivalent form of politeness, and it serves its turn. "Pleasure," he said, and walked off.

Work Points:

The western red-footed kestrel, the pygmy falcon, the pale chanting goshawk, the spotted eagle owl.

Abdim's stork, the wattled plover, the lesser flamingo, the white pelican, Burchell's sand grouse, the yellow-billed hornbill, the gray hornbill, the red-billed hornbill, the ground hornbill, the African hoopoe, the ground-scraper thrush.

The plum-colored starling, the paradise flycatcher, the white-backed mousebird, the black-faced babbler, the bare-cheeked babbler, the masked weaver and its nests.

The golden-breasted bunting, the gray lourie, the crimson boubou, the black-collared barbet, the white-bellied sunbird, the purple roller, the blue waxbill, the red-billed firefinch.

The white rhinoceros, the black rhinoceros, the black-backed jackal, the wild dog, the rock dassie, the slender mongoose, the yellow mongoose, the banded mongoose, the suricate.

The steenbok, the klipspringer, the Damara dik-dik, the springbok, the black-faced impala, the gemsbok, the kudu, the eland, the pangolin, the giraffe.

The warthog, the porcupine, Burchell's zebra, Hartmann's mountain zebra, the sable, the antbear, the brown hyena, the spotted hyena, the cheetah, the lion, the leopard, the caracal, the aardwolf, the elephant.

Beetles too numerous to name.

We stayed on the farm for three days. I came to know a little of the rhythms of the working day: the women who swept and did the washing, the men who tended fence and herded cows. Their names were Lesley, Mona Lisa, Anastasia, and Sarah and Isaskar, Erastus, and Johannes. Sarah, an old Herero woman, wore four layers of clothing and smiled at me toothlessly and kept an eye out for the children underfoot. Little Ralphie and four-year-old Colin—the son of Erastus and Mona Lisa—racketed around on tricycles and played complicated games with oranges and plastic tractors and swords.

Patti H. owns a ranch in Montana and is an accomplished horsewoman; she assessed the herd of Brahma bulls and compared American and Namibian management techniques. She and Hörst engaged in lengthy discussions as to the weight of cattle and comparative feeding and fencing and veterinary practices, and she said how much these systems resembled those of Montana, how very much this landscape reminded her of home. From time to time Hörst went out hunting in order to provide the workers and their families with meat, and on Monday afternoon we traveled with him in the open bed of the Land Rover truck; he was looking for oryx, he said.

An oryx or gemsbok stands four to five feet high; it has a pair of straight horns ringed at the base. Of the members of the antelope family, it occupies the middle ground—larger than the diminutive dik-dik and the springbok, smaller than the eland and the kudu. The gemsbok runs effortlessly, compactly, skimming over the veldt, and when viewed in profile can seem to have only one horn. This, and its compelling beauty—"oryx" and "auroch" are linked words—has rendered it a stand-in for that mythical creature, the unicorn. To hunt and slay a unicorn is to court disaster, and I had mixed feelings about our pursuit.

Nonetheless we banged and rattled down the farm roads, past leaning termite hills and grazing cows and kori bustards and a secretary bird. The kori bustard is heavy-bellied, slow to fly, and the secretary bird (so named because of a feather dangling like a quill pen from its crest) stared us down from a safe distance; warthogs scuttled over the road—a mother herding children—and through the open sections of the fence. We crossed an empty riverbed and ducked free of acacia tree branches and their eye-impaling thorns. The hunting dog, Tigger, whined and strained against the leash; I clipped it to a crossbar on the truck.

Hörst had been a professional butcher and is a licensed hunter and crack shot. "To be a licensed professional," he said, "you have to make your target at 150 meters; I myself manage 300." He smiled. He sat in the passenger seat, protective earphones slung around his neck and holding his Austrian rifle: well oiled, a heavy Mauser 30.01, with telescopic sights. Danielle had spotted an oryx gone lame—a wound on its left hind leg festering—and this was the beast we attempted to cull, but we were downwind of it and the oryx scented us and lumbered out of range. "If not today, then next time," said Hörst. "I won't forget, I promise."

Then he spotted several gemsbok in the road. Irresolute, they scattered, some disappearing in the acacia thickets, some returning to the waterhole they'd left. Silently Hörst slipped free of the truck and climbed a hill above the water hole and, following the rim of it, disappeared from sight.

We heard a shot, a second shot, and by the time I reached him he was cutting the animal's throat. It bled redly into the sand. Tigger was sniffing it, licking its neck, and we let down the tailgate and lifted up the body and, twenty minutes later, were back at the farm buildings and swinging wide the gate.

A practiced dance ensued. Hörst unloaded his kill on a platform where men waited with hoses and knives. Isaskar sliced the withers free and attached hooks to the gemsbok—smaller-seeming now when dead—and raised the body on a chain until it hung waist-high above the concrete floor. Then the process of skinning and butchery began. Two men removed the Land Rover and started hosing down its blood-stained bed; another with a wheelbarrow was stacking and removing cuts of meat. The air was cool, the risk of spoilage small, but they worked with brisk efficiency—hanging haunches, ribs, and steaks from hooks in a refrigerated chamber, separating out the brains and offal and meat to be smoked while the dogs of the compound—two Jack Russells, a Rhodesian ridgeback—watched. Twenty more minutes and nothing was left; little Ralphie rode his tricycle in circles and the rinsed barrow dried in the sun.

On our fourth morning at the farm, Hellmut F. arrived. He is a near neighbor and part-time safari guide; he would lead us west and south. Counting Hellmut himself, there were eight of us now, and we required two vehicles: a white 1991 Toyota 4 × 4 Land Cruiser—most cars are white in this country, to reflect the heat and reduce the look of dust—and a remodeled 1975 Ford 250 truck. This is Hellmut's conveyance of choice, and in it he had packed four tents, eight sleeping bags and mattress rolls and blankets—these summer nights south of the equator can approach the freezing point—as well as food and drink and cooking equipment and camping tables and eight chairs, and he had packed the whole with attention to detail and balance. The chassis had been lovingly repainted a light blue.

His windshield sports three decals: TASA (Tour and Safari Association Namibia) FULL MEMBER; EURO CRITI-MED with numbers to call in case of medical emergency, and an emblem of a kudu head, its rack enclosing the legend: NAMIB-IA *Professional Hunting Association, fully licensed guide.* The truck's roof is white, and on it Hellmut had welded platforms to hold the metal tables and two spare Dunlop 750–16 eight-ply tires—both of which, in the first days of driving, he would need. Forward on the roof, he had reserved a space where he himself sleeps in a pup tent; there were water tanks for storage—one of cold water and one warmed by proxim-ity to the truck's exhaust pipe—and a generator and a refrig-erator and repair kits and pumps and shovels. Our bags went in the Toyota, and we followed where he led.

Hellmut is a large man, full-stomached, fifty-two years old, with a gray beard and head of black hair. He was born in Okahandja and—with the exception of a year in Iraq, working on Caterpillar tractors, and a stint in Brazil—has lived in Namibia all his life. His wife, Gabriela, grew up in Brazil and for three years he worked there for her father, farming ("He cheated me," said Hellmut, "he promised me 300 cows and I got nothing, nothing!"); now he supplements his income as a cattle farmer by taking customers out on the road. His card reads: *Wir sprechen Deutsch and Portuguese.* He traveled, he told me, two months every year; when fin-ished with us, for example, he would accompany three Ger-man ladies to Botswana and "Vic Falls." "I don't mind," he said. "It doesn't bother me."

Little bothers him, or so it would seem; when George pro-posed a stop, he said, "It's your safari, not mine." Our desti-nation was a warehouse outside the city of Windhoek, where we purchased bottled water and soda and wine. Hellmut himself prefers to drink beer and had brought along a case and—limiting himself to a smoke every hour—packs of cig-arettes. "I stay with the cars," he announced, and sat on the Ford's running board in order to discourage theft; he ex-tracted a cigarette from his shirt pocket and leaned back and lit up. The Namibian dollar—pegged to the South African rand—is seriously undervalued, and American money goes a long way; the best wine on the shelf cost less than ten dollars per bottle. We laid in an ample supply. Then, painstakingly, our purchases were checked off against receipts by an armed guard at the checkout line; the parking lot too was guarded by soldiers with guns. Next we made for the town of Rehoboth and left paved roads behind.

In 1969 there were forty miles of paved highway in Namibia; now that number has been multiplied, and exponentially. The roads are well maintained. But nine out of every ten hours, we drove on hard-packed, unpaved surface—two-lane highways, gravel roads, then trails, then rutted, rock-strewn paths—and following Hellmut's dust. We stayed sufficiently behind to avoid the dust but not so far as to lose track of him entirely; at intersections, idling, he would wait. From the time I checked my watch, the first oncoming traffic we encountered—a single car—took four hours to appear.

We had booked a campsite in Maltahöhe, at Tsauchab River Camping ground, and would stay there for two nights. The Namib Naukluft Desert Park—our destination next morning—is an ancient, empty place of red dunes and drifting sand; Sesriem Canyon guards its entrance, and far beyond the entrance rolls the sea. But the campground itself is a stretch of rock and thistle; a few goats grazed, and Johan S.—who owns the land and registered our vehicles—waved us toward "the Fountains" five kilometers away. By his tractor shed he kept an ostrich, and there were barn cats and a mongoose playing at his feet; there was a collection of rifles inside, and old farm implements, and the whips called skjamboks; the skin of a black mamba snake had been nailed above the postcards and water and tobacco and insect repellent for sale. The snake's skin was six feet long—small, Eddie assured me—and when I asked if the black mamba is alert this early in the season, Johan said, "Not very. Only a little." He smiled. "You must pay attention more to scorpions. About the black mamba there's no point to worry; if it bites you and you have the venom"—he snapped his fingers—"ten minutes, you're dead."

In the language of the Hottentots, "Namib" means "empty place"; this was that. A pile of upright stones, we learned, was the grave of one of the "old people," or San; they are buried on their feet, as if preparing to rise. Baboons surveyed our progress past yellow spray-painted trail markers; Hellmut's left rear tire—I was close enough to see it now—had sprung a leak. In the morning he would pump it up and, when the thing deflated again, replace it with one of his spares.

"Moonscape," said Patti.

"The end of the earth," Eddie said.

"The Fountains," once we reached them, were slime-encrusted standing pools, green-mantled until wintertime and rain. At length we came upon a stopping place, a fenced enclosure with an outhouse and a round stone structure with a sink and a fire pit where we would fry our meat. In silence we arranged our tents and sleeping bags; we then met Marcus, the custodian of "Fountains." He brought wood. He wore blue coveralls and a lumberjack's shirt and Yankees baseball cap; he sported a gap-toothed grin and cigar and shook hands repeatedly all around. A Herero with six children, he lived, he told us, just down the way, around the bend of Zebra Trail.

"Welcome, welcome Mister from America," he said, "the Misses too."

In this low place night came quickly; by six o'clock it was dark. We ate eland steak and potatoes baked in foil and drank several bottles of wine; the boys petitioned for glasses and drank too. James would be departing for college two days after his return, and his parents argued as to whether it was best to prepare him for school by letting him have wine or not, or if he should drink beer. "Whatever you say," Hellmut said.

I am a touch typist and I regaled the company by typing in the dark. "Tell me a story," I said, and they offered stories I took down. Patti talked about the different ways that elk are killed—how wolves, bears, and mountain lions stalk and attack their prey. Bears cuff the cow and eat the tongue and udder and bury the rest till it rots; a mountain lion lands on top and mangles the entire cow; by contrast, wolves hamstring their supper and eat while it's alive. Eddie told a story of a patient in Johannesburg and how his patient died. Eddie thought it might have been salmonella, but it was arsenic poisoning—or so insisted the dead man's daughter—and they exhumed the body and several lawsuits ensued. Danielle's father had been a doctor too, and she told the story of how when she was young the two of them witnessed an accident—an overloaded truck upended on a mountain slope like the one we had just now descended, spilling thirty-seven bodies down the scree. "He could save none of them," she said. "'Poor fellows,' I remember, that's what Daddy said. 'Poor fellows,'" repeated Danielle.

The guinea fowl were clamorous; baboons, too, fussed and clattered in the trees. "They are hoping for our garbage," Hellmut said. There were high winds all night long. After a period of fitful sleep, we proceeded at dawn to Sossusvlei in the Namib Naukluft Desert Park. Those who camped at the mouth of Sesriem Canyon had been driven back by the force of the wind, and in Capetown to the south the storm carried snow in its teeth. The Tsauchab River, gone underground, emerges in the desert at times of heavy rain. In the park itself were warnings that four-wheel drive is required, and before we engaged the Toyota's front wheels we did get stuck in ruts.

But the dunes were spectacular: high, windswept, roseate, unending. The flat-caked mud beneath us had been a water basin, clearly, and there were footprints embedded from when the mud dried hard. Eddie is a naturalist; he showed me snails and the sand track of snakes and the telltale marks of a jackal's rear paws and which feathers came from which birds. At one o'clock we returned to the truck and had lunch in its shadow, eating sandwiches and apples and peanuts and drinking tea from a Thermos. Eddie pointed out a tok-tokie beetle, its black carapace so low-slung that when tapped against the ground it sounds a reverberant "tok." The sand grew hot. What wore this landscape down is time: the unremitting light, the drifting grains. Where I have walked such dunes before—or anything approaching them—it's been with the sense of water waiting at the farther side. Indeed, the Atlantic does break on these shores, but many kilometers distant; what roared here was the wind.

Henno Martin and his friend Hermann Korn were conscientious objectors during World War II; appalled at the prospect of "the mass suicide of civilized peoples,"[3] they fled to the Namib desert and hid from authorities there. *The Sheltering Desert* is Martin's reconstruction of their two and a half years as "Robinson Crusoes in the Namib," and it makes for a riveting read. They had a truck and ammunition and a shortwave radio; they had some chocolate and a camera and a faithful dog named Otto and very little else. They rationed supplies and stowed the truck in order to avoid police; bit by bit and week by month they came to understand the desert's harsh imperatives. They taught themselves to stalk, kill, skin, and smoke their prey; they fashioned bullets and dental fillings and traps for birds and fish. These two German geologists learned to live and kill as the San people had for centuries, and they evaded detection. It's not so much that the Namib wastes are trackless—footprints and tire tracks last in the sand—as that caves and canyons and far-flung water holes and overhangs lend protective coloration to the man who hunts escape; a needle in a haystack would be easier to find.

We drove to the south of Kuiseb Canyon and walked along a trail announced as leading to Henno Martin's camp. The way is neither steep nor long, but after fifteen minutes winding past the scree and stone I was as lost as those who tried to roust out the deserters in 1942. Carp Cliff—so named because the men found carp there they could net and eat—is a mere indentation in an expanse of rock. Their hiding place has been preserved—a wall of stones to blunt the wind, a fire pit for smoking meat—and it is appalling to think of calling it home.

Martin and Korn did so nevertheless through winter and summer, drought and cloudburst; they deferred to leopards, outwitted hyenas and baboons, ate zebra and oryx and quail. They carried *biltong*—dried meat—and water and foraged for honey and salt. When they had slaked their need for drink and food they engaged in earnest Germanic speculation as to the nature of man's nature—the "bare, forked animal" and his propensity for self-destruction; they conducted geological surveys and admired the sunsets and played the violin. They tried to grow carrots and radishes and broke camp twice—once for lack of water and once for fear of discovery—and patched their shoes with rubber and listened to broadcasts announcing the assault on Russia and praising Hitler and Rommel. They came close to outlasting the war.

In the end, however, a severe vitamin deficiency forced Korn to turn himself in. By the time they were imprisoned, they needed a hospital; vitamin B extract turned the trick. As Martin puts it in his epilogue:

> We were charged with a whole battery of offences: failure to notify our change of address, failure to pay our dog licence, failure to pay motor-car tax, failure to hand in our radios according to the war-time regulations, the illegal possession of arms, the shooting of game without permission, and so on. We might have got it hot and strong, but the magistrate who tried us showed understanding for our adventure and sympathy for our position, and merely imposed a series of small fines. A friend of ours lent us the money to pay, and that was that.[4]

Work Points:

A sign to a lodge called UTOPIA.

The town of Solitaire. A gas station and shop for provisions, an advertisement for Taffel Beer and tomorrow's prizefight: Larry Holmes vs. Battling Brown.

The "Old People" slaughtered for sport.

On Main Street in Karibib, a Western Restaurant with a sign for a BEER GARDEN, TELLER ESSEN; T-BONES;

SALATE, AND WINDHOEK LAGER. The Club Western Gambling House.

The Rider Memorial statue in Windhoek commemorating
German soldiers killed in the Herero and Nama wars.
Some 65,000 of the 80,000-strong Herero died.

Towns we drove through: Otijwarango, Usakos, Otavi,
Bullsport, Naukluft, Tsumeb, Outjo, Omaruru.

Towns we did not: Oshakati, Ondangwa, Swakopmund,
Maltahöhe, Lüderitz, Walvis Bay, Keetmanshoop,
Oranjemund.

The mineral wealth: diamonds, uranium oxide, copper,
granite, marble, zinc, gold, silver, salt. Tantalite,
columbite, vanadium, sillimanite, kyanite, lithium,
germanium. Caesium, cadmium, beryllium, wolfram,
lepidolite, amblygonite, petalite.

Kaokoland, Damaraland, Hereroland, Namaland, the
Caprivi Strip.

The Kalahari Sands Hotel in Windhoek; Christuskirche,
the city's Evangelical Lutheran church, consecrated
in 1910.

Kobos, Klein Aub, Lepel Store, then south again through
the Remhoogte Pass and west on C-14.

The Skeleton Coast.

The "Rostock Ritz" is, as its self-conferred title suggests, a
luxury hotel. This meant there was hot water and a restaurant
and mosquito netting coiled above each bed. A generator and
solar panels provided electricity; the rooms were faced with
stones and blended into the landscape; dead trees as a design
motif had been embedded in cement. There were peacocks by
the reception area, waiters in uniform, a swimming pool. The
menu was capacious, promising calamari and ostrich and
crocodile and escargot; when I asked to taste the ostrich,
however, our waiter announced smilingly that neither ostrich
steak nor crocodile nor squid would be available tonight.

In truth, the "Ritz" was welcome after our nights spent
camping, and the shower worked. The Rostock mountain

range—a contraction for "Rotstock," red mountain—rings the hotel's hilltop perch, and its emptiness feels absolute: sand blowing over ditch and shrub, a night sky fat with stars. The hotel manager, a young man called Hein, took us next day to see cave paintings in the Rostock Range. It was an hour's drive, and he discoursed on the virtues of his Toyota truck, its wheel base, its suspension and springs. "How old do you think I am?" Hein asked. "How old do you imagine?" When I ventured, "Thirty, thirty-two?" he answered, triumphantly, "Twenty-three."

An empty riverbed had high-piled brush against the road, and he said, "You can't imagine what it's like when the rains come, the river breaks these trees like matchsticks in the period of flood. A week ago," said Hein, "we had a German staying here, and he said, 'I'll bring you a chainsaw the next time, I promise,' and I laughed with him and said, 'What would you need a chainsaw for in Rostock? There are no trees to cut.' These branches come from upriver, from hundreds of kilometers away."

The track grew steep. The truck leaned crazily, careening over boulders; we climbed to the base of a pass. Hein turned off the engine and distributed water and beer and said, "Now, please to follow me," and we made our slow way up behind him to a ledge beneath an overhang. "Here are the paintings," he said. He waved his hand expansively at smudges on the low red rock, and it took some time to distinguish what was man-made and intentional: a series of images of ostrich, oryx, springbok, and running women and men.

We bent to study them. The overhang was low. A person standing upright to paint could not have been more than five feet tall or, possibly, these artists worked while on their knees. Hein extracted some beads from the sand: finely wrought ostrich eggshell circlets he had buried by a rock so as to keep them safe for the next tourist visit. The largest of the circlets was smaller than my fingernail, and they were thin to the point of translucence: five hundred would have made a necklace, two hundred a bracelet for a small-boned wrist. Our guide next produced a wax-coated twig from a

Bushman candle tree, which he proceeded to light. It smelled like incense, sputtering to flame.

We do not know the purpose of this art. It has something to do with celebration and the hunt—but whether as a propitiary image of the souls of beasts new-slaughtered or an emblem of those soon to be killed, it's impossible to tell. Cave paintings in the south of France are dark and difficult of access; this place was remote, admittedly, but open to the elements and not in the same way hidden; it felt as though the men and women who once came to worship would have done so unafraid. Priapic men are leaping; women too. Shaman shapes festoon the wall.

"I knew you by your shadow" is the traditional greeting of the San people; "I saw you from afar." These diminutive folk enlarged themselves in pictographs; they tower over eland, wildebeest, and even a rhinoceros. An ostrich is dancing; a springbok pronks. On one outcropping there are muddied crisscrossing lines, a series of hands imprinted on the ledge of rock as though by children finger-painting. Hein shook his head and said, "Perhaps the painters were confused; who knows what they were smoking or what they drank?" In the thirty decorated feet of stone, I counted more than two hundred such images: a cluster of animals running, a teeming population where all is absence now.

The palette is various; though faded today, it would have been vivid when first—unnumbered centuries ago—applied. From hematite or limonite the painter got his reds, yellows, purples, and browns; from kaolin (as well as, plausibly, from the digested bone fragments of raptors) she got her white, from charcoal, the gray and black. These pigments would be mixed with fat—most frequently the marrow of the eland, whose long shoulder blade also provided material for the bone burins used in etchings. Stone chisels and porcupine quills served their turn; the color was rarely applied by brush—more often the artist used fingers or sprayed paint on by mouth. When brushes were deployed, they came from bird feathers or animal hair; grass and bone too were pressed into service, and pigment could be stored in ostrich eggshells or hoof sheaths or the sheaths of horns.[5]

This art reports on and was nourished by the hunting life: thirst, hunger, accident, the skills of stalking, the pleasures of a feast. Was there a special caste of artisans, a particular initiation rite for those of the San people who produced these images? Were they in fact "special" or was this a widespread skill, an attainment as common as the knowledge of where to find water or the efficacy of herbs? As Jon Manchip White reports, in his travel book on Namibia:

> The last attested example of the high art of the Bushman appears to date from 1869, in which year George Stow watched a Bushman delineate a group of Boers on horseback. It is to Stow that we owe the first copies of Bushman painting, and the first attempt at a definitive study: and it is Stow who has recorded the death of the last Bushman artist. He tells us that the artist was shot down in Basutoland during the course of one of the murder commandos which brought about the systematic extinction of the Bushman nation. Hanging from a zebra skin belt around the dead man's small body were the horn pots containing his colours.
>
> It is seldom that one is able to date with such cruel finality the ending of a great school of art. . . . It had survived for a hundred thousand years. It could not survive the last two centuries. It could not survive the spears of the Hottentots and Bantu, nor the rifles of our own white grandfathers, the first lethal promptings of the cult of order and progress stirring in their hearts.[6]

Our fifth night on the road, we reached Tsaobis Leopard Nature Park. Its site is unprepossessing, eleven kilometers from nowhere, with an abandoned airplane landing strip and hangar in a field. Though its brochure declares the park is "Situated half-way between Windhoek and Swakopmund on the scenic C-32 road," the nearest town is Karibib and the road a washboard where Hellmut had to change another flat. There are dry riverbeds and camel-thorn trees and bush-littered hills: fine camouflage for leopards on the prowl.

This reserve, however, is devoted to the care and feeding of animals that have been maimed or somehow incapacitated and would perish in the wild. Several come from zoos where they were abused; a vervet monkey had been sold to the camp by Angolan mercenaries years before. Its mother had been shot. Solo, it swung from roof to wall and platform of its wire pen. The vervet can be taught to steal and therefore is much prized. There were a pair of cheetahs, a pair of leop-ards, a pair of caracals, and two aardwolfs; there were moun-tain zebras in the riverbed just beyond the fence.

An English volunteer who introduced himself as Paul de-scribed the animals' hunting habits and ranked them in terms of success. The aardwolf, he said, is nocturnal and shy; it eats tens of thousands of termites but won't do so in plain sight. The caracal will kill for sport; farmers hate the caracal, it kills more than it eats. "Your cheetah," said Paul, "that's an ex-cellent stalker, but in spite of its great speed it needs to start no more than thirty meters from its prey. It's not strong enough to rival, say, a lion or keep hyenas at bay, so I would put it near the bottom of the solo predator's list. Wolves, for example, hunt in packs, and that's a separate proposition and requires separate skills. Your wild dog," he continued, "now that's a remarkably astute hunter, but it too is collective and hunts in a pack; the leopard is a solitary predator and stows its prey in trees. That way it can return to feed and there'll be something left. I've seen a leopard carry an eland twice its weight and hang it over a branch in a tree, and once I saw it with a burden too heavy to carry, so it stopped and gutted the eland and left the entrails and inedible parts at the tree's base and then carried the carcass on up. Your leopard—" he repeated, "to my mind the leopard's the king of the jungle, the most successful predator of all."

The young proprietors of Tsaobis, Andres and Tana, had a three-month-old son called Louie, and they welcomed us with unfeigned enthusiasm: a chance for adult talk. They were starved for conversation, they said, what is a life without books? "It would be a satisfaction," they said, "if you joined us at seven tonight."

The meal was excellent. The few other campers in the park had elected the "self-catering option" and were missing what turned out to be a feast. Tana had baked bread and squash and two varieties of chicken and a chocolate cake; the red wine was abundant, and Louie suckled and slept. We sat at table for hours while Andres elaborated on his dream of olive groves, his plan to plant that hillside there and his certainty that in five to ten years there'd be an olive yield. Wind lifted the reeds of the building's thatched roof. He would corner the market, Andres declared, or at least a significant proportion of the demand for olive oil; "Why not Namibian olives," he asked me, "instead of Italian or French?"

"How would you irrigate?" I asked. "Where would you find the water?" He smiled. "How would you package and export the yield? Is there," I asked him, "a mill nearby, or at least an olive oil press?" Dismissively, he waved his sunburned hand. "An olive tree," I said, "can live for centuries. They're slow to start; you don't want to wait till you're fifty to sample the first crop."

But none of this dissuaded him; he leaned back in his chair, eyes shining, and pointed to the Southern Cross. "Just there," he said, "just on that hill, that's the grove I'm planning to establish first; you must come back and see."

Helmut is at ease with silence; he drank his beer and yawned. Eddie, too, kept his own counsel, and stared at the night sky. But the demon of argument was on me; I kept attempting to explain that olives were a chancy crop, that I had lived in olive country in Provence, and though he might possibly manage with goats, an olive grove takes time. Those caged animals, I tried not to say, were emblems of their owners, and he didn't want or shouldn't plan to make himself a hostage to the vagaries of weather or long-term investment that might fail to yield. "Come back," he said, "in five years' time and see."

Baboons cavorted where I lay, kecking and wahooing and tattooing drumrolls on the water tower. For hours on end, or so it seemed, I listened to them serenade the guinea hens, the guinea hens respond in kind; and all night in my fitful sleep I dreamed of sirens, traffic noise, the comforting bustle of town. "Pleasure," said Andres at breakfast. "Pleasure," we said, and drove on.

That night we made a campsite underneath Gross Spitz-koppe—a set of craggy peaks that Hellmut seemed to favor. It is a difficult mountain to climb, its summit first scaled only in 1946. We drove past domelike Pondok Mountain and Klein Spitzkoppe and found campsite #11 under a rock ridge. Hellmut produced "spaghetti Bolognese" as a special dinner treat, heating water and sauce on his camp stove; the meatballs were oryx, he told me, which is why the flavor was so much better than what you get in Italy. "Have you ever been to Italy?" I asked, and he said, "Of course not, no; why would I go to Bologna when I eat spaghetti here?"

We saw zebra in abundance; ostriches, too. Over dinner there was conversation on the character of zebras, their in-tractability. "Like mules, they are," said Hellmut. "You mustn't trust a zebra, you have to stay clear of its teeth. Hooves, too; a zebra breaks a lion's jaw with just a single kick."

"Myself," said George, "I trust the ostrich less." If an ostrich attacks you, they told me, what you must do is lie down. Its kick is what you have to fear; its toe can ram through metal, but it has to raise its foot to kick, and if you lie down you're all right. "Except if it sits on you," said George. "And that isn't very much fun." "Not so serious," said Hellmut. "After twenty-four hours of sitting you can wring its neck. It's permitted to strangle an ostrich. If you must. . . ."

At the crossroads past the campground at Spitzkoppe, there was a market for stones. This meant that men and women with children displayed a clutch of colored rocks and crystal on trestle tables in the sun, and they assured us of the rarity and excellence of what they sold. The stones were black, red, green, and yellow, and Danielle knew what she was looking for and bargained happily, at length. There ensued a complicated etiquette of call and answer, bid and counterbid; in the process of reaching a sum with which she was satisfied she switched from English to German, then to Afrikaans. I marveled at the language skills of these analphabetic people, the way they were so fluent when discussing *beauty, value, price,* but would no doubt be tongue-tied by a noncommercial text. This is as true of children in Turkey or Thailand as of the children who hustled us here; once the transaction was finished, they resumed their game of soccer in the hot white dust.

I tried to send some postcards to America. It proved difficult, however, to find stamps—and though Patti and I bought a whole sheet of stamps with giraffes gazing soulfully left to right, no one seemed certain how much postage would be required. We asked at three separate places and were told three different amounts. At the "Rostock Ritz," for example, the woman said, "We could mail them for you. But we go to Swakopmund only once a month and were just there. It would be much better if you mail the cards yourself."

Post offices were few and far between and, when we located them, shut. It occurred to me that in my first ten days of travel I had met no other Americans, and this was a pretty good working definition of distance: when the people who sell postcards do not know how much to affix for mail to the United States, the long arm of our nation's reach has outstripped its grasp. They did know what it cost to send a card to Germany; they gave me the precise amount for South Africa and Egypt. But America was anybody's guess. At last, in the Okahandja Post Office, having waited in a slow-moving line of soldiers cashing chits, advancing past a gathering of old Herero women who stared at me, incurious, I was informed by the postmistress how many stamps it takes. Her number contradicted what we'd been told before; I bought a second sheet.

Work Points:

The steering wheel on the right-hand side of the truck.
   The English way of driving, here, on the left-hand side
   of the road.
The airport exit door marked NOTHING TO DECLARE.
The marinade for oryx is peri-peri sauce. Biltong strips like
   pemmican or salt pork. Braided lengths of meat.
Eddie: "Once you've been in the bush you need to return.
   It gets to you, gets under your skin like these burrs."
A swarm of bees by the farm gate, another at our window.
On the rondavel wall, a gemsbok skull and a kudu skull.
Bright bougainvillea by the eating porch.
The hand-cranked telephone.
Jackals by the water hole. "And some are rabid," says
   Danielle, "and must be shot on sight."
Community nests. The weaver bird nests built on tele-
   phone poles. The copper wire, because of its value, is
   at risk of theft.
If you project a circle made by the Southern Cross and
   its two pointer stars, then the center of that circle will
   always be due south.
The termite hills.
If you point the "12" of your watch directly at the sun,
   the hour hand points north.
Tigger is part Dalmatian, mostly German short-haired
   pointer. Two years old.
"I shall live and die in Namibia," Renate says. "Of this I
   have no doubt at all, of this there is no question." Then
   she asks of each of us, "For tomorrow morning, do you
   prefer coffee or tea?"
One warthog called Harley Davidson because of the size of
   his horns. They look like handlebars, and though he'd

be a trophy head, he's left unharmed: a yield of, if not
domesticity, old age.
    "*N'importe où hors du monde.*"

Our second visit to Erichsfelde feels, if not routine, familiar,
and that night we eat again beneath the orange tree. We have
returned for provisions and mail and because Eddie must
leave. We will stay in touch, we promise, and exchange ad-
dresses. We have shared a tent and hikes and stories and I
like him very much and know with certainty I will never see
him again. "Work requires it," he says, departing for Johannesburg. "Tomorrow there's a hospital meeting I can't af-
ford to miss."

Isaskar hopes to be a licensed hunter, and under Hörst's
close tutelage has passed the written test. He still has to practice his shooting, however—particularly in front of
strangers—and on the day we return to the farm Hörst asks if
we would come along, once more in the truck bed, to witness
a hunt. Once more we stand on sacks of grain, distributing
mineral supplements and salt licks to the cows, filling their bar-
rels with feed. Once again Tigger strains at the leash, scenting
the prospect of game, and once again we sight an oryx past the
water hole. Hörst spots it and points and stops the truck; taking slow aim—too slow, it seems—Isasker shoots.

The oryx bolts. The shot was a long one—140 meters,
says Hörst, looking glum. "Now we shall have to see what
happened and look, if we hit him, for blood." "I think he
shot too high," I whisper to Andrew. "He missed." It's late
afternoon, not two hours from dark, and if indeed the oryx
has been wounded, he will be hard to track. The ground is
dry and hard and when the two men find a spot of blood it
does not elate them; a large animal can run for miles with a
gut shot or a surface scratch, and in these acacia thickets
might be suffering unseen.

Andrew and I stand in the truck bed with Tigger. He
whines and yelps and barks. For twenty minutes we hear

nothing but the dog, the crows, the rising wind; we talk of what will happen if indeed it grows too dark to see and who would walk the miles to the farm and who would remain with the truck. Then Isaskar comes back, running, and drives us clatteringly across the empty riverbed and the brush-thick veldt. The oryx is dead, huddled beneath a camel-thorn tree; it had been shot through the lung. "I could not ask for more," says Hörst, "if everybody shot that way . . ." and reaches down and slices off the creature's genitals and hands them to Isaskar. From what appeared at first a failure and an embarrassment his student has emerged triumphal, and Isaskar is elated, clearly, but trying not to show it. We wrestle the large corpse into the truck bed, and half an hour later it is being butchered and the truck hosed down.

At five o'clock, with the workday complete, the people of Erichsfelde gather at the storeroom—a large locked closet by the garage—and Renate distributes soap and shoe polish and cooking oil and makes a note of who has purchased what. Then we distribute our gifts. In preparation for the journey, I had packed T-shirts and sweaters and ballpoint pens with which I did not intend to return; George had brought a bag of shoes, and Patti some blouses and skirts. Renate has already made an allocation—ten piles of cast-off clothing—and that afternoon we present them to the workers. It is a complicated occasion. Danielle makes a speech, in Afrikaans, thanking them all for their help and saying how we have brought them these gifts from America and hope they may be of use. Unsmiling, they step forward—first Isasker, then Erastus, then Lesley and Johannes and stooped, retired Marcus, then the women: Anastasia, Mona Lisa, Sarah—and retreat with their new old clothes. I have brought a Superman T-shirt, a T-shirt from a lawn watering service, one each from *The New York Times* and *Seventeen* Magazine and the Bennington Writing Workshops and a poetry slam in Ann Arbor: a dozen fresh-pressed cast-offs with English-language slogans that none of these people can read. It is, George assures me, largesse. It is an act of generosity not condescension, but it feels very much like the latter. As darkness falls, we disperse.

Etosha National Park, a game preserve larger than Rhode Island, is our final destination; we drive to and then across it for three days. The word "Etosha" means "Great White Place," and the Etosha Pan—blindingly empty and white—heralds a prehistoric waterway and was a delta once. When the rare rains come, flamingos materialize, and I have seen photographs of thousands of pink flamingos on what now is a mud-caked, hardscrabble expanse: no water, only the illusion of it in the dry shimmering air. The land is organized for the animals' sake, not for the sake of the humans who watch; there are strict rules of the road. At peril of expulsion from this Eden, you must stay on the network of dirt tracks that lead from water hole to water hole and remain inside your car.

There are three places to spend the night within the park: Namutoni, Halali, and Okaukuejo, proceeding east to west. The first is a fort, established at the turn of the twentieth century in order to control the spread of rinderpest; the second, a resort so named because of a German hunting song whose chorus is "Halali"; the third, a ring of bungalows beside a water hole. On the drive from Namutoni we see elephants in quantity—so many I lose count of them—and they cross the path we travel on not fifty meters away.

The water hole in Halali hosts elephants and rhinoceros and giraffes. At nine at night the world is dark, but there are spotlights focused on the water hole, and the animals are used to them and do not seem to mind. There are benches for the visitors and posted warnings to stay silent and alert. Park lore has it that, some years ago, a tourist fell asleep on a bench and was eaten by a lion marauding there at dawn. But here we have safety in numbers, some sixty or seventy humans in ranked rows above the water hole: a pack observing in shared silence while elephants gambol and drink. The white light leaches color from the scene. I watch the people watching: lovers, parents with their children, a group of teenagers from Italy who had set their camp up raucously but now are standing rapt.

On our last afternoon in Etosha, fifteen kilometers distant from the lodge at Okaukuejo, we see a pride of lions stalking prey. This is at the Okandeka watering hole; we have been told that lions have been sighted and drive out to see. There are oryx and springbok and zebra; there are wildebeest and warthog and kudu and giraffes. But the game is skittish, refusing to drink, for downwind of the water hole a lion prowls and upwind the pride lies in wait. It is hard to spot them: motionless, ears twitching, the color of the sand and grass, but we find and count them not fifty meters from the road: six heads behind a hillock, seven, eight. A lion sleeps twenty hours a day; these creatures are awake.

We cannot remain there, however, for it is growing dark. The gates are locked at sundown, and the rules of the park are absolute: if you violate the curfew—no one can be on the roads from sunset to sunrise—you are thrown out. So we can only briefly watch them while they prepare to kill.

Our guide in Okaukuejo is a friend of Hellmut's, Irmgaard, a woman in her forties, and she says, "Let's come back at dawn, at first light let's return." She is a handsome woman, garrulous; she was born in Okahandja and tells us about her two daughters and how they are at boarding school but come home every weekend and how the members of the family all get along; she speaks about her time in Windhoek, working at a disco, and how she met her husband and curtailed a trip to Munich and how many brothers her husband has and how many people work on his farm; she asks do we have allergies and do we mind if she smokes? "Not inside the car, of course, I never smoke inside the car," says Irmgaard, "and I'd never cheat on my husband because first of all I don't want to and in any case, in this little country everyone would know. They don't have enough to think about," she says. "These people poke their noses in everybody else's business, and they talk and talk."

At dawn, however, she stays silent and drives on the *qui vive*. The lodge gates opened at six. A giraffe is silhouetted by the rising sun, in a far field, and when we return to the watering hole there are lions on the road. We count eight. They swagger heavy-bellied past us, unperturbed; the dark-maned leader lurches by, not ten meters off, and vouchsafes us no glance. At the Okandeka water hole his pride has gathered, waiting, and he selects a hummock and lies down.

By a camel-thorn tree are jackals, hunched above a carcass, but there are so many clustered to the lion kill I cannot tell what animal they feed on. "Oryx," says Irmgaard, and points, and indeed there is a horn. "Perhaps the one we saw last night. The old one on the hill, remember? The one who was standing alone?"

The jackals finish feeding and trot off. There are red bones protruding, a single horn above the grass, and then the pied crows arrive. Next they will take their turn.

You are reading this letter, I hope. I write on my old Olivetti, in the cold dawn; the roosters have been clamoring since five. The Rhodesian ridgeback too—the dogs have the run of the compound at night—is restive: prowling, barking, troubled by a jackal or a baboon. This farm is half the world away from where I imagine you reading: winter to your summer, drought to rain. Soon Erastus will arrive and light the fire in the donkey—a metal water boiler—and there will be hot water and I'll shave. Soon there will be tea and toast and, our bags packed, departure: the hills of Ombutozo giving way to Okahandja and then Okahandja to Windhoek and then, again, a plane.

Mona Lisa sweeps the path. Light increases; the roosters subside. I have met no native here who has visited America—a few have gone to Germany—and New York or San Francisco is as unimaginable to them as, brief weeks ago, was the town of Solitaire to me. You are standing with the chair pushed back, reading words like "kudu," "biltong," "Rostock," and with a second set of eyes can see what I am looking at: the cactus, the acacia, and the cherished orange tree. This land God made in anger is a place of beauty, bounty, and you who study maps can chart it now a little, I believe. I am glad to be returning, glad to have been here. "Pleasure," says Hörst, and we leave.

Northern Lights

A salient feature of the landscape is its light—the long "white nights," as Doestoevski called them, and then the wintry dark. He was writing of St. Petersburg, the temptations of desire, and how the stars give way to snow yet both can cause night blindness. We imagine what cannot be seen. Those northern representations of the world of love in drama—think of Ibsen, Strindberg, Bergman—offer a spate of inward-facing scenes. In part, perhaps, because the landscape of theater is contained—hemmed in by rooms and curtains—it's easier to represent a passionate encounter that takes place *within*.

There are exceptions to this rule, productions such as *The Wild Duck* and *Peer Gynt* or *Wild Strawberries* and *Smiles of a Summer Night*—set more in exterior and cinematic terms than in those of the stage. By and large, however, the action of Scandinavian drama is circumscribed by walls. Think of *Hedda Gabler* or *Miss Julie* or the light of Bergman's films: the settings are domestic—hedged against the elements, lamp- or candlelit. The characters remain inside, whether in a doll's house or, as with John Gabriel Borkman, self-confined upstairs. When Chekhov describes *The Cherry Orchard* or Turgenev *A Month in the Country*, there's the constant presence of the drawing room, though from time to time the actors exit left to stroll or shoot. The Norwegian novelist Pär Lagerkvist sets his characters adrift—in such exile narratives as *The Dwarf* and *The Death of Ahasuerus*—but this is to deny them the comforts of the hearth. The wanderers who seem lightly disguised self-portraits in such Knut Hamsun novels as *The Road Leads On* or *The Growth of the Soil* leave society behind; when they venture forth, it's at risk. And the Icelandic laureate, Halldór Laxness, does much the same; in books like *Independent People* and *The Fish Can Sing*—for which he earned the Nobel Prize in 1955—landscape forms a crucial part of the characters' behavior, their tales of love and loss.

I like to believe this is true: Søren Kierkegaard, a very private man, went out into the world each day—and did so very publicly. He made a habit, it would seem, of stopping at cafés, at parties and receptions and the opera, and making sure, for an hour in the afternoon, that everybody in society saw him table-hopping, handshaking, clapping acquaintances on the back. As a result, he acquired a reputation as a gadabout and not someone bent to the desk. Which he was, of course, and obsessively, for the other twenty-three hours—but locked away secure in the knowledge that nobody knew he was working. This seems to me emblematic of the literature, its "fear and trembling unto death": a brief fierce daylit foray and nightlong isolation. From the very earliest texts up to the present moment, these men and women have been haunted: mist monsters, changelings, dragons, and unquiet spirits everywhere. It's not an accident that man meets ghost at Elsinore; those fog-wreathed battlements belong to the chill north. . . .

In a survey of northern literature, one must border-cross, traversing boundaries as did the early wanderers, not those stay-at-homes who limn the maps. The lines between the Swedish and the Danish, the Norwegian and the Finnish, the Icelandic and the Estonian are difficult to draw. As Aristotle long ago informed us, we only note the differences in those things that are in essence similar; we might compare a horse and cow but not a horse and tree; we might compare a car and truck but not a truck and lake. So what we have to start with are the Eddas and the sagas—when the people of the region were by and large seaborne and on the move.

Though we know little of its origins, we know the genre had been established by the ninth century; there are some 250 named poets as well as anonymous rhymes. The verse form is called "skaldic," a close relative of our own Anglo-Saxon—word cluster–based, alliterative—and it has two varieties: a lengthy celebration of a lord and a brief occasional stanza on a single theme. These belong to the oral-formulaic tradition, harp-thwacked: a set of stories told and passed from generation to generation around the guttering flame. . . .

Mr. or perhaps Ms. Anon are the authors of these poems, and rarely does an individual claim sole ownership. But one was a national singer, well known at the time and much acclaimed—the way Dante Alighieri would be soon, or Geoffrey Chaucer the next century. Snorri Sturluson lived from 1179 to 1241. Of an aristocratic and cultured family, he was raised in southern Iceland; he visited Norway and Sweden and stayed there for some years. His prose Edda is a compendium of skaldic tradition—the legends and folktales, the narratives of discovery and settlement. He codifies the Nordic myths as well as the ensuing history of kings.

Sturluson provides us, in effect, with a road map of the great void, Ginnungagap, of Ygdrassil, the mighty tree and World Ash whose branches hold the sky. He names the residences of the gods, Valhalla, the hall of the slain, and those figures of mythology—Odin, Thor, Loki, Frey—we recognize today from Wagner and *The Niebelungenlied*. These are not the gods of Olympus; they're less capricious and meddle less down here below, but they too have their progeny and present celebrants; think of J. K. Rowling and J.R.R. Tolkien. . . .

Such literature is powered, it would seem, by two equal and adjacent motives. The first is pride. The bard reports on the recent or receding past, and the message is, in effect, we *are* a people and these are exploits to remind you of, the history of our ancestors. The Eddas memorialize hardships endured and the triumphs that ensued. Yet oral-formulaic reportage is more or less coeval with the fear of loss—the waning of tradition and the feeling that old ways are at risk and *need* to be preserved. This second impulse—preservation—is not so much at odds with the first as complementary to it, and here the individual does enter in. A consciousness obtains, an individual shaping of the collective tale. Soon or late a scribe appears and, in castle keep or monastery or the halls of academe, starts to write things down. . . .

In this regard, for example, my Penguin Classics edition of *Hrafnkel's Saga and Other Stories* opens with the assertion that "Nothing is known of the authorship of *Hrafnkel's Saga*." Yet the editors proceed to a lengthy discursus on and consideration of the thirteenth century, the "Golden Age" of saga writing, and "the outstanding qualities of realistic fiction in mediaeval Iceland." There are pastoral society stories; there are four—*Hreidar the Fool, Halldor Snorrason, Audun's Story,* and *Ivar's Story*—that describe the adventures of Icelandic poets and peasants at the royal courts of Norway and Denmark. These stories, however, according to the authoritative Herman Palsson, "were probably written by authors who had never visited Scandinavia and had therefore no first-hand knowledge of the physical and social background to the incidents they describe."[1] It's possible to make things up as well as write them down. . . .

One wanderer combines all this, and he's one of the first great travel writers, both participant and scribe. Imagine for a moment that Homer sang about his *own* exploits in the Trojan War or that the *Chanson de Roland* came to us from someone who survived the battle of Roncesvalles. It's personal attestation mixed with the communal memory; it's a blend of borrowed finery—the Beowulf story looms large in this adventure—and homespun account.

We know the author's name, or an approximation thereof. In June of 921 A.D., the Caliph of Baghdad sent Ahmad

Ibn Fadlan as ambassador to the King of the Bulgars. This emissary was away for three years and never in fact fulfilled his mission; instead he fell in with a company of Norsemen and had many adventures among them. He'd planned, or so it would seem, a brief foray north, but life among the Vikings was a good deal more than he had bargained for, and he reported on it at length. To posterity's great benefit, Ibn Fadlan was literate, and the account of his journey still makes an excellent read.

We know almost nothing about him personally. Ibn Fadlan was educated, courtly, and—judging by his exploits—could not have been very old. He tells us he was a familiar of the caliph, whom he does not appear to admire. Much of what he found in the north struck him as vulgar, barbaric, even obscene, but he wastes little time in indignation; having expressed disapproval, he goes right back to unblinking reportage. He is interested in both the everyday details of life and the beliefs of the people he meets. And he reports on what he sees without condescension. In a vivid formula, we are told he was able to "draw sounds"—by which is meant, of course, the art of penmanship, much more prevalent in Baghdad than in Bergen at the time. The bulk of his account rings true, and whenever he reports by hearsay, he is careful to say so. He is equally careful to specify when he has been an eyewitness; routinely he uses the phrase, "I saw with my own eyes."

This information derives from a contemporary version of the text. Michael Crichton, in 1976, produced a novel he called *Eaters of the Dead*[2] based on the manuscripts of Ibn Fadlan; there was a more or less faithful movie—also produced by the admirable Crichton—called *The Thirteenth Warrior*, and starring Antonio Banderas as a not-quite-convincing sheik. It had the obligatory cameo by Omar Sharif and a shot or two of desert sands; mostly it takes place on ice floes and caves from the Universal backlot. There's a lot of mist and mud and sword fighting and an extravaganza of special effects. Faithful to Ibn Fadlan's adventures only at a great remove, the film nonetheless manages to convey both a sense of distance and the imperative of translation—that transforming process of strangeness grown familiar that heralds the genre as such.

The original manuscript has long since disappeared; to reconstruct it we must rely on fragments preserved in later sources. They date from the eleventh to the sixteenth century, and several versions have survived. A good deal of scholarship has been expended, for example, on the matter of "the Bulgars"; Ibn Fadlan may have gone to Russia—he does use the words "Rus" and "Vyking"—since most of his mission was nomadic, on the move if not the run. His account of a "Rus" funeral is justly celebrated, and it tells us a great deal about the burial practices of the time. This is cultural anthropology of the very highest order:

> I saw with my own eyes how the Northmen had arrived with their wares, and pitched their camp along the Volga. Never did I see a people so gigantic: they are tall as palm trees, and florid and ruddy in complexion. They wear neither camisoles nor caftans, but the men among them wear a garment of rough cloth, which is thrown over one side, so that one hand remains free.
>
> Every Northman carries an axe, a dagger, and a sword, and without these weapons they are never seen. Their swords are broad, with wavy lines, and of Frankish make. From the tip of the fingernails to the neck, each man of them is tattooed with pictures of trees, living beings, and other things.
>
> The women carry, fastened to their breast, a little case of iron, copper, silver, or gold, according to the wealth and resources of their husbands. Fastened to the case they wear a ring, and upon that a dagger, all attached to their breast. About their necks they wear gold and silver chains.
>
> They are the filthiest race that God ever created. They do not wipe themselves after going to stool, or wash themselves after a nocturnal pollution, anymore than if they were wild asses. (32–33)

These Northmen are by their own accounting the best sailors in the world, and I saw much love of the oceans and waters in their demeanor. Of the ship there is this: it was as long as twenty-five paces, and as broad as eight and a little more than that, and of excellent construction, of oak wood. It color was black at every place. It was fitted with a square sail of cloth and trimmed with sealskin ropes. The helmsman stood upon a small platform near the stern and worked a rudder attached to the side of the vessel in the Roman fashion. The ship was fitted with benches for oars, but never were the oars employed; rather we progressed by sailing alone. At the head of the ship was the wooden carving of a fierce sea monster, such as appears on some Northman vessels; also there was a tail at the stern. In water this ship was stable and quite pleasant for traveling, and the confidence of the warriors elevated my spirits. (51)

Also, Herger explained to me that in this North country the day is long in the summer, and the night is long in the winter, and rarely are they equal. Then he said to me I should watch in the night for the sky curtain; and upon one evening I did, and I saw in the sky shimmering pale lights, of green and yellow and sometimes blue, which hung as a curtain in the high air. I was much amazed by the sight of this sky curtain but the Northmen count it nothing strange. (54)

Of the table of Rothgar I shall say this: that every man had a tablecloth and plate, and spoon and knife; that the meal was boiled pork and goat, and some fish, too, for the Northmen much prefer boiled meat to roasted. Then there were cabbages and onions in abundance, and apples and hazelnuts. A sweetish fleshy meat was given me that I had not tasted before; this, I was told, was elk, or rain-deer.

The dreadful foul drink called mead is made from honey, then fermented. It is the sourest, blackest, vilest stuff ever invented by any man, and yet it is potent beyond all knowing; a few drinks, and the world spins. But I did not drink, praise Allah. (96)

Let us fast-forward now, a thousand years. Here's another admirable writer, another displaced person, though her most famous wandering and relocation took her from the North Country south. The Baroness Blixen, known more widely as Isak Dinesen, wrote in *Out of Africa* about what it meant to travel in the reverse direction. I like this crisscrossing pattern: Ibn Fadlan goes north, Dinesen south, a millennium later, and makes a life in Kenya managing a coffee plantation. The movie based on that experience takes full advantage also of star power—in this case that of Meryl Streep and Robert Redford—and the wide-screen land- and skyscape so suitable to film.

But the enduring work is Dinesen's northern, inward-facing fiction: the stories in *Winter's Tales* or *Anecdotes of Destiny* or *Seven Gothic Tales*. Her final publications, *Last Tales* (1957), *Shadows on the Grass* (1960), and *Ehrengard* (1963), are, as one critic puts it, "further collections of stories in which a sophisticated, aristocratic wit is put to work on a tradition of writing that has suffered from the lack of it."[3]

Again the sensibility is highly refined and ironic; again the scenes portrayed can be primitive in the extreme. It's the surprising juxtaposition of an educated author—like Ibn Fadlan, trained to "draw sounds"—and raw surrounding circumstances that gives these tales their force. We're told that Isak Dinesen, for the last years of her life, subsisted—if one can call this a subsistence diet—on oysters and champagne. Or, as Miss Malin Nat-og-Dag (the ancient noblewoman marooned and soon to die in "The Deluge at Norderney") puts it:

And when I have, in my life, come nearest to playing the role of a goddess, the very last thing which I wanted from my worshipers has been the truth. "Make poetry," I have said to them, "use your imagination, disguise the truth to me. Your truth comes out quite early enough . . . and that is the end of the game."[4]

I own a Modern Library edition of *Seven Gothic Tales*, published in 1934 and with an introduction by Dorothy Canfield Fisher. Ms. Fisher announces up front that she can report nothing at all about Dinesen, using the masculine pronoun to describe the writer and leaving the issue of identity alone; as recently as 1934, therefore, our author's name and gender were unknown. Blixen had written under the *nom de plume* of Osceola for Danish periodicals; a later pseudonym would be Pierre Andrézel, for her 1947 novel, *The Avengers*. This hunt for anonymity seems apposite; it's not merely that Karen Blixen wanted to protect her privacy and family reputation, it's that she tapped into the taproot, as it were, of the storytelling past: the bardic impersonal voice.

Consider the opening sentence of "The Roads Around Pisa." Though she borrows from gothic tradition and what I've just called the impersonal voice, no one else could have written this line: "Count Augustus von Schimmelmann, a young Danish nobleman of a melancholy disposition, who would have been very good-looking if he had not been a little too fat, was writing a letter on a table made out of a millstone in the garden of an *osteria* near Pisa on a fine May evening of 1823."[5]

And here's the first sentence of "The Supper at Elsinore": "Upon the corner of a street of Elsinore, near the harbor, there stands a dignified old gray house, built early in the eighteenth century, and looking down reticently at the new times grown up around it." Three members of the De Coninck family gather in their ancestral home; two of them are maidens grown old; a third—their younger brother—is a ghost:

When they turned their heads a little, they saw their brother standing at the end of the table.

He stood there for a moment and nodded to them, smiling at them. Then he took the third chair and sat down, between them. He placed his hands upon the edge of the table, gently moving them sideward and back again, exactly as he always used to do.[6]

This brother, Morten, and Hamlet have a good deal in common. "He had been, indeed, in Elsinore, as another highborn young dandy before him, the observed of all observers, the glass of fashion and the mold of form. Many were the girls of the town who had remained unmarried for his sake."[7] Dinesen uses this setting—as with others in her *Gothic Tales*—to meld the actual and the invented, the real and the surreal.

Finally, here are the first paragraphs of her short story, "Sorrow Acre," from the collection *Winter's Tales*:

The low, undulating Danish landscape was silent and serene, mysteriously wide-awake in the hour before sunrise. There was not a cloud in the pale sky, not a shadow along the dim, pearly fields, hills and woods. The mist was lifting from the valleys and hollows, the air was cool, the grass and the foliage dripping wet with morning-dew. Unwatched by the eyes of man, and undisturbed by his activity, the country breathed a timeless life, to which language was inadequate.

All the same, a human race had lived on this land for a thousand years, had been formed by its soil and weather, and had marked it with its thoughts, so that now no one could tell where the existence of one ceased and the other began. The thin grey line of a road, winding across the plain and up and down hills, was the fixed materialization of human longing, and of the human notion that it is better to be in one place than another.

A child of the country would read this open landscape like a book.[8]

The author then proceeds to limn the land in terms of peasantry, clergy, nobility; she moves from field to church to manor house. The prose conveys deep knowingness, a set of worldly ironies:

The big house stood as firmly rooted in the soil of Denmark as the peasants' huts, and was as faithfully allied to her four winds and changing seasons, to her animal life, trees and flowers. Only its interests lay in a higher plane. Within the domain of the lime trees it was no longer cows, goats and pigs on which the minds and the talk ran, but horses and dogs. The wild fauna, the game of the land, that the peasant shook his fist at, when he saw it on his young green rye or in his ripening wheat field, to the residents of the country house were the main pursuit and the joy of existence.

The writing in the sky solemnly proclaimed continuance, a worldly immortality. The great country houses had held their ground through many generations.[9]

"Worldly immortality" will be, in this story, at stake; the ground beneath the "great country houses" commences soon enough to shake. The "old lord" who owns the property receives a visit from his nephew Adam—the name is not accidental—who may or may not inherit the place, and whose modern knowledge (he has arrived from England and is planning a trip to that brave new world, America) causes him to question Eden and its ancient ways. The precipitating action has to do with a worker accused of arson; the old lord's barn has been burned. This boy's mother pleads for his life; she swears that he is innocent while others protest his guilt.

Godlike if not Solomonic in his judgment, the lord of the manor proposes a test. "That gave me an idea. I said to the widow: 'If in one day, between sunrise and sunset, with your own hands you can mow this field, and it be well done, I will let the case drop and you shall keep your son. But if you cannot do it, he must go, and is it not likely that you will then ever see him again.'"[10]

The bulk of the story consists of the old woman's loving labor, her solitary scything of the field of rye. The old lord watches; so do his peasants and his bailiff and his horrified nephew, Adam, from sunrise to sunset while Anne-Marie toils alone. It is a superhuman task; three men might manage in one day, or one strong man in three. Uncle and nephew engage in disputation as to the nature of belief, the possibility of progress, the question of whether tragedy or comedy best describes the human condition and, conversely, that of the gods. Servants bring their master hot chocolate in the morning, food and Rhenish wine at lunchtime, his full court dress at dusk. As night falls, the old woman completes her final cut and, "softly and lingeringly, like a sheaf of corn that falls to the ground," she embraces her son and dies.

Let this brief discussion end at story's end:

> The people who had followed Anne-Marie all through the day kept standing and stirring in the field for many hours, as long as the evening light lasted, and longer. Long after some of them had made a stretcher from branches of the trees and had carried away the dead woman, others wandered on, up and down the stubble, imitating and measuring her course from one end of the rye field to the other, and binding up the last sheaves, where she had finished her mowing.
>
> The old lord stayed with them for a long time, stepping along a little, and again standing still.
>
> In the place where the woman had died the old lord later on had a stone set up, with a sickle engraved in it. The peasants on the land then named the rye field "Sorrow-Acre." By this name it was known a long time after the story of the woman and her son had itself been forgotten.[11]

Such a summary cannot do justice to the force of parable, the weight of circumstance and philosophical import of this narrative. It has metaphoric resonance, a way of staying in the mind "a long time after the story of the woman and her son had itself been forgotten." The land with the stone and sickle engraved on it, the *agon* played out between ruler and ruled, the clash of value systems between the traditional and new—all these signal artistry the more complete because unobtrusive. As in another of her great short tales, "Babette's Feast," we have a plenitude of paucities stored up as celebration; at its best, the work of Isak Dinesen will last,

I'd guess, as long as that of the medieval tale tellers whose work she emulates.

Iceland today is by all measures the most literate of societies—the highest proportion of books bought and read, the largest number of translations per capita—and one has the sense in this part of the world that language truly matters and literacy counts. For those in the book business, Norway, Sweden, Denmark, Finland, though admittedly a much smaller market than North America, are nonetheless more profitable and reliable; during the long white nights and inside the dark houses, people *read*. And while it's no longer the case in Russia that language is subject to to state censorship, it's easy to remember how powerful had been the secret text, the banned book, and the subversive document: when writers set down their stories at risk, the results are doubly—trebly—valued.

The reverse is also true. Pushkin was a member of the imperial inner circle, Tolstoi a member of the ruling class, and their proximity to power adds power to their work. One of the important gestures, early on, of Catherine the Great was her sponsorship of Diderot's *Encylopedia*; she underwrote his massive compilation and—relatively cheaply—earned herself the sobriquet of patron of knowledge and art. It's a smart way to spend imperial cash; that blind bard near the fire may make you famous later on—or turn you into a villain if you turn him away from the door.

A consistently best-selling Scandinavian author is Hans Christian Andersen. This nineteenth-century Dane, whose father was a shoemaker and whose mother was almost illiterate, wrote fairy tales of enormous popularity; "The Princess and the Pea," "The Emperor's New Clothes," "The Little Mermaid," "Thumbelina," and the rest are part of our cultural heritage now. He represents a strain that Karen Blixen also incorporates: the fantastical, the otherworldly brought down to this earth. No literature of which I'm aware is more at home with fable; the magical and the homespun narrative share, as it were, one roof. This is another way of saying that Ibn Fadlan's mist monsters stalk the pages equally of Andersen's stories and Dinesen's tales, and the thousand years between them seem but an eye blink, a wink.

The third leg of our triangular exploration is a tale of exile, both actual and imagined. Narrow-seeming on the surface, *Pale Fire* is a wide book. Vladimir Nabokov deploys several genres—poetry, fiction, a parody of scholarship, the whole paraphernalia of critical commentary—within a seamless whole. This is travel writing in the largest sense: traversing space and time in an invented country, yet suffused throughout with yearning for the real world left behind.

Though an extravagantly clever work of words—full of wit and parody and trickster turns and complicated patterning—it's powered everywhere by a heartsore need to recapture via language what has been lost in life. Much of his *oeuvre*, indeed (from *Speak, Memory* to *Ada*) has at its core this same fierce nostalgia: a retentive inventiveness that both preserves and transforms. And with the lack of reliability that signals Nabokov's narrator throughout, he does what he says he won't do: "I have no desire to twist and batter an unambiguous *apparatus criticus* into the monstrous semblance of a novel."[12] So insists Kinbote. More precisely, perhaps, his "onlie sole begetter" does the reverse: making an ambiguous novel of a monstrous critical apparatus and twisting it into a mirroring Möbius strip—the "semblance" of Zembla itself.

This final "northern light" was born in St. Petersburg, Russia, in 1899. His grandfather had been minister of justice under two czars, and his father a celebrated statesman of the liberal group before the revolution. Because of the series of events that transformed that town into Leningrad, Nabokov became a lifelong expatriate; in 1917 his family left Petersburg and two years later left Russia for good. His father—anticipatory shadow, perhaps, of Gradus and Shade?—was assassinated in Berlin in 1922. A wanderer thereafter, the artist spent much of his productive career in the United States writing *Lolita* and other novels (as Kinbote puts it, "Hurricane *Lolita* swept from Florida to Maine!") while teaching at Cornell.

Nabokov lived his final years in Switzerland, in the Grand Hotel in the town of Montreux: a lepidopterist of distinction, a chess player of determination, a critic and translator and short story writer and novelist and crank *par excellence*. He spoke English with an atrocious accent and wrote it surpassingly well. He loved his pages, not his page boys, in contrast to Kinbote. As his biographers report, Nabokov was—although imperious and absent-minded and a snob—not mad. At sixty-one years old, he produced a book about a sixty-one-year-old writer sheltered and praised by the academy; there the resemblances end.

A point to make, to start with—so obvious it need not be belabored, but worth noting nevertheless. Like his predecessor Joseph Conrad (a Pole, of course, not a Russian, and one to whom our author vigorously denied any connection), Nabokov wrote in something other than his native tongue. These two great practitioners of English came to it tardily, if not late; they would have learned, though not spoken, the language while young. Nabokov did in fact publish several early books in Russian, then translated them—together with his son Dmitri—and started to compose in English well before *Pale Fire*. But Russian came first for him, then French, and German too; in an essay on translation (composed when he was a present past master of the tongue) the writer had this to say: "The English at my disposal is certainly thinner than my Russian; the difference being, in fact, that which exists between a semi-detached villa and a hereditary estate, between self-conscious comfort and habitual luxury."[13]

If Nabokov's English is indeed "thinner than my Russian," then God help us all. I know no other English so thick. One might even argue there's a certain overanxious grappling for precision, a lack of fluency with the demotic; he's ill at ease with slang. But this makes it all the more comical—

and a source of great amusement in a novel such as *Pnin*—
when his foreigners mangle the language. John Shade writes,
"the grand potato," and Kinbote calls it "an execrable pun"
on Rabelais, who went in search of death, "*le grand peut-
être*"; this is the sort of word play or word golf that, in *Pale
Fire,* abounds.[14] Kinbote habitually confuses and conflates
his referents or makes outright reversals—spider, redips, T.
S. Eliot toilest, and so on. Here, for example, he translates
Queen Disa's letter: "'I want you to know that no matter
how much you hurt me, you cannot hurt my love,' and this
sentence (if we re-English it from the Zemblan) came out as:
'I desire you and love you when you flog me.'"[15] Everything
is subject to translation in the expatriate kingdom of words.

Samuel Beckett provides a contrary instance, and a consequential one; at a certain stage of his career he left fluency behind; finding it over-easy to make sonorous puns, he chose
to write in a non-native tongue and renounced English in favor of French. Beckett's exile was, however, self-imposed,
not enforced by a totalitarian regime, and his landscape of
verbal displacement is in almost every way the opposite of
Nabokov's: abstract, uncluttered by the time he turned to *En
Attendant Godot.* If nothing else, *Pale Fire* is a prime example of the primacy of verbal skill in the game of articulate art.
Or, as Kinbote tells his friend—who fears to violate that in-
trusive thing, reality—"'do not worry about trifles. Once
transmuted by you into poetry, the stuff *will* be true, and the
people *will* come alive. A poet's purified truth can cause no
pain, no offense. True art is above false honor.'"[16]

Nabokov's imagined artist is briefly convinced of an afterlife;
he has an "out-of-body" or "near-death" experience and sees
a tall white fountain when he has a heart attack. The doctor
assures him that he hasn't died, is only "half a Shade," but
then he reads an article about a half-dead woman also brought
back from the brink, who also saw that fountain. Shade tracks
her down and gets, as it were, no satisfaction; then he visits
the reporter who publicized her story. This latter says, oh,

they printed it wrong; her word was "Mountain," not "fountain." In pentameter and rhyming couplets, John Shade (as well as, of course, his progenitor) delivers an uninflected paean to the pleasures of such mistake making in the service of precision:

> Life Everlasting . . . based on a misprint!
> I mused as I drove homeward: take the hint,
> And stop investigating my abyss?
> But all at once it dawned on me that *this*
> Was the real point, the contrapuntal theme;
> Just this: not text, but texture; not the dream
> But topsy-turvical coincidence,
> Not flimsy nonsense, but a web of sense.
> Yes! It sufficed that I in life could find
> Some kind of link-and-bobolink, some kind
> Of correlated pattern in the game,
> Plexed artistry, and something of the same
> Pleasure in it as they who played it found.[17]

A principal strategy in this novelist's game—the "link and bobolink"—is that of the untrustworthy or unreliable narrator. It's a technical device, organized by irony, in which there's substantial distance between the thing said and the thing meant—or, more intricately, between what the speaker sees and we as audience perceive. Sometimes this can be serious, dramatic or even melodramatic: the good guy who protests his decency turns out to be a villain, the woman who calls herself fallen turns out to be a saint. The strategy depends on a first-person narrator; it doesn't work in the omniscient authorial voice or at a third-person remove. All mysteries (*Pale Fire* is to some degree a mystery; at any rate, it depends on riddle solving) require puzzling out; we believe A is the killer but he turns out to be the victim, and B, whom we thought blameless, is in fact the one to blame. . . .

This kind of manipulation derives from the author's arrangement of facts, not the character's; as soon as we have a first-person account, the issue of trust enters in. So an un-

trustworthy or unreliable narrator such as Kinbote can declare, "My neighbors love and want to see me" when we as
readers understand they shut the door and hide; he'll say,
"They swear *by* me" when we know they're swearing *at*.
Consider Humbert Humbert in *Lolita* and his protestations
of devotion to the nymphet he corrupts; there are two sides
to each story, and we read them both at once.

Nabokov is never so simple, however, nor so reductive as
I've just been. There are more than two sides to each story;
Humbert Humbert truly loves the girl, and Kinbote is more
than the mere thief of John Shade's manuscript; he's also its
enabler. Further, and though he cannot bring himself open-
ly to admit it, Kinbote is not deluded as to his social standing
in the town he's tried to make a home, and does not fail to
recognize the poet's wife's dislike. Just as people used to argue whether the story of Humbert Humbert and Lolita was
of old Europe corrupting youthful America or of depraved
America seducing innocent Europe, so one could argue at
some length about which of these two characters is the sun
and which the moon. The matter of mistaken identity in *Pale
Fire*, of doubles and imposters, of secret passages and staged
escapes, belongs to burlesque, if not farce. For the prevailing
mood is humorous; this is a comedy, not tragedy, and the
death and disaster and carnage are reported tongue in cheek.

Consider a single example; there are a thousand such.
Lines 96 to 98 of the titular poem read:

> The human skull; and from the local *Star*
> A curio: *Red Sox beat Yanks 5–4*
> *On Chapman's Homer*, thumbtacked to the door.[18]

This is vintage Nabokov as Shade. We don't know what
the town might be (most likely an inexact replica of Ithaca)
or if there was a local paper called the *Star*. It's probable the
Red Sox—King Charles's disguise, escaping, is red—once
beat the Yankees by that score; it's possible they had a batter
called Chapman and he hit a home run. The notion of the
"*Star*" in any case attaches to the firmament; "the human

skull" induces us to meditate on mortality. The passage starts (l. 86), "I was brought up by dear bizarre Aunt Maud . . ." and catalogues her "realistic objects" fondly; Shade keeps her room intact. And there's an ease with the American scene— its paperweights, its thumbtacks—that bespeaks a native speaker; this one's modeled, more or less closely, after Robert Frost. But Kinbote in his commentary gets it all wrong, while accusing the printer, or even Shade himself, of having done so. Kinbote's annotation reads:

Line 98; On Chapman's Homer
    A reference to the title of Keats' famous sonnet (often quoted in America) which, owing to a printer's absent-mindedness, has been drolly transposed, from some other article, into the account of a sports event. For other vivid misprints see note to line 8o2.[19]

John Keats, of course, is another poet dead untimely, and the "famous sonnet" to which Kinbote refers is "On First Looking Into Chapman's Homer." Those fourteen lines begin, "Much have I travell'd in the realms of gold" and end with an explorer "Silent, upon a peak in Darien." The poem takes as its subject the aesthetic marvel of the Homeric landscape and how the poetic imagination—in this case, that of the stay-at-home, bedazzled Keats—can, via translation, take wing. Kinbote knows nothing about baseball or that those who play it in America might be called "the Yanks," and his homer is uppercase, a blind Greek bard; Barry Bonds hit more than seventy lowercase versions of the word a few seasons ago. So we as readers can make fun of what the critic calls "drolly transposed" and turn to the next series of "vivid misprints."

Yet John Shade himself had gotten the joke, which is why he responded to "dear bizarre Aunt Maud" and her having thumbtacked that article to the door of her room. So a prior character finds the phrase "Chapman's Homer" amusing, as does the poet who recalls her, as does the novelist who invents them both—while a third personage, invented too, complains about the printer of "some other article." We as readers therefore get to eat our cake and have it; Kinbote makes a reference, then fails to make another (the one that Shade was making and Aunt Maud first noticed) till the juxtaposition of them all becomes prismatic, doubly and trebly reflective. In his foreword, Kinbote suggests:

> Although those notes, in conformity with custom, come after the poem, the reader is advised to consult them first and then study the poem with their help, rereading them of course as he goes through its text, and perhaps, after having done with the poem, consulting them a third time so as to complete the picture.[20]

The end of the foreword sounds a clarion call:

> Let me state that without my notes Shade's text simply has no human reality at all since the human reality of such a poem as his (being too skittish and reticent for an autobiographical work), with the omission of many pithy lines carelessly rejected by him, has to depend entirely on the reality of its author and his surroundings, attachments and so forth, a reality that only my notes can provide. To this statement my dear poet would probably not have subscribed, but, for better or worse, it is the commentator who has the last word.[21]

If we do the rough arithmetic, only a quarter of what Kinbote writes takes the poem "Pale Fire" as its topic. I mean by this that, though he announces early on that his job will be to serve as commentator-exegete, what Kinbote in fact produces is a history of his own quasi-mythical escape from Zembla and the ensuing search. The Extremist assassin Jakob Gradus, the actor Odon, the various enthralling gardeners and boys in boots, the sad queen Disa and *her* double, Fleur de File: all these have nothing obvious to do with what Shade wrote. Nor do the conversations of the poet and his obtrusive narrator-neighbor; they are "bobolinked" by contiguity not continuity, and tell a very different kind of story than do the opening lines.

But those commentaries have, it seems to me, a common theme and subject: death. This is Shade's concern throughout "Pale Fire," and it arrives in fictive actuality before the poem's done. It's Kinbote's concern throughout—his lengthy descriptions of the assassin, his long discourse on suicide, his ruminations on religion and the afterlife: all are variations on the theme of that "waxwing slain" we read about in the poem's first line.

The book's last note makes this confusedly clear. Here the diction borrows from (or more properly echoes) the dying speech of an alter ego, Clare Quilty, in *Lolita*: it's direct address, and slangy in a way that reminds us how much of a performer our Kinbote-Botkin has been:

> Many years ago—how many I would not care to say—I remember my Zemblan nurse telling me, a little man of six in the throes of adult insomnia: "*Minnamin, Gut mag alkan, Pern dirstan*" (my darling, God makes hungry, the Devil thirsty). Well, folks, I guess many in this fine hall are as hungry and thirsty as me, and I'd better stop, folks, right here.
>
> Yes, better stop. My notes and self are petering out. Gentlemen, I have suffered very much, and more than any of you can imagine. I pray for the Lord's benediction to rest on my wretched countrymen. My work is finished. My poet is dead.
>
> "And you, what will *you* be doing with yourself, poor King, poor Kinbote?" a gentle young voice may inquire.
>
> God will help me, I trust, to rid myself of any desire to follow the example of two other characters in this work. I shall continue to exist. I may assume other disguises, other forms, but I shall try to exist. I may turn up yet, on another campus, as an old, happy, healthy, heterosexual Russian, a writer in exile, sans fame, sans future, sans audience, sans anything but his art.[22]

The referent is not only Clare Quilty but also the Savior who sacrificed himself for "my wretched countrymen." Equally seriously, and equally tongue in cheek, there's an echo of Jacques's "seven stages of man" from *As You Like It*, with the last taking place "sans teeth, sans eyes, sans taste, sans everything." And the "healthy, heterosexual . . . writer in exile" is Vladimir Nabokov himself, pulling the strings of his puppets so they may entertain. If we substitute for Shakespeare's "everything" the "anything but his art," we get a sense of how all-inclusive are the claims this "old, happy . . . Russian" makes for artistry and how confident he feels of fame and future audience.

And the literal last words of the index and novel are these: "*Zembla,* a distant northern land."[23] On page 45 of my *Britannica World Atlas*, at the top of the map of the top of Russia, there's an island called "Novaya Zemla" that curves enticingly, as King Charles says, and from which it might be possible to glimpse the motherland. So this inventive text, wherein an exile dreams of home, concludes with the difficult heights to which the book attains:

> Several trails cross the mountains at various points, and lead to passes none of which exceeds an altitude of five thousand feet; a few peaks rise some two thousand feet higher and retain their snow in midsummer; and from one of them, the highest and hardest, Mt. Glitterntin, one can distinguish on clear days, far out to the east, beyond the Gulf of Surprise, a dim iridescence which some say is Russia.[24]

Novaya Zemla is an actual island on an actual map.

On Daniel Martin

To call John Fowles neglected is to stretch a point. His is a career most other authors would envy; he's widely read and praised. Born in England in 1926, Fowles studied French at Oxford, then taught in France and Greece; he calls Lyme Regis home. A brief listing of achievements—though the final tally's not yet in—will suffice. His books are many and various; as of this writing, they number sixteen. These include a collection of poems (*Poems*), a book of philosophical aphorisms (*The Aristos*), several discussions of landscape and of local history (*The Tree, The Island, Shipwreck, The Enigma of Stonehenge, A Short History of Lyme Regis,* etc.), a novella and short stories (*The Ebony Tower*). Recently a collection of essays (*Wormholes*) has appeared, and there's the *jeu d'esprit* of *Mantissa,* a literary parlor game played by postmodernist rules.

It is as a novelist, however, that Fowles stakes his principal claim. His first three novels were best-sellers in America and each became movies thereafter. Terence Stamp, Anthony Quinn, and Meryl Streep bodied forth the title roles of *The Collector, The Magus,* and *The French Lieutenant's Woman,* respectively; Laurence Olivier played the protagonist of "The Ebony Tower" for a television production. It's possible, indeed, that Fowles's reputation as a "serious" writer has been somehow undermined by commercial success; in England particularly, it would seem—though I have only anecdotal evidence for this—he's thought of as a popular and therefore unimportant writer. "If you're so smart, why ain't you rich?" gets transformed in critical discourse to "If you're so wealthy, how could you be smart?" and Fowles has been devalued in part because of fame.

Further, for medical reasons, his rate of output has been reduced; there's been silence of late from Lyme Regis. Our anticipatory expectation—what will he turn his hand to next?—no longer feels keen-edged. Death engenders re-assessment; Fowles is alive but in retreat, and at the moment there's a trough, not crest, in the wave of attention.

The purpose of these pages is to reverse that reversal and to propose a corrective. As John Gardner (another novelist whose reputation has declined) wrote in 1977, "John Fowles is the only novelist now writing in English whose works are likely to stand as literary classics—the only writer in English who has the power, range, knowledge, and wisdom of a Tolstoy or James."

Gardner issued this panegyric in a review of *Daniel Martin* for the *Saturday Review*. He calls Fowles "a master stylist" with "the talent, much underestimated these days, for telling suspenseful, interesting stories." And he calls "*Daniel Martin* . . . a masterpiece of symbolically charged realism: every symbol rises, or is made to seem to rise out of the story."[1]

I agree. Unlike the previous novels, *Daniel Martin* (1977) has not been made into a film—though it is concerned with Hollywood and its eponymous hero writes screenplays. Perhaps because the "scenarist" himself displays such manifest scorn for the world of the movies, that world reciprocates. Too complex and inward-facing for ready "translation" to celluloid, *Daniel Martin* resists easy access; indeed, that is part of its protagonist's intention and part of its author's point. I have the impression—again anecdotal—that those who buy a book by Fowles tend to purchase *The French Lieutenant's Woman* rather than *Daniel Martin*; those who teach him teach the former in preference to the latter; this transatlantic book about Englishness is more referred to than read.

The longest and most ambitious of Fowles's novels is, however, a major work and, to my mind, his best. Seven hundred pages of purposively meditative prose, it begins with a clarion call: "Whole sight, or all the rest is desolation."[2] And in the final scene—when Dan confronts the great Rembrandt self-portrait in the gallery at Kenwood—that assertion is repeated. In what may be a tip of the cap, via its "flagrant Irishry,"[3] to Joyce's *Finnegans Wake,* the concluding phrase of the book declares the work's circularity. The creator says of his character, "his ill-concealed ghost has made that impossible last his own impossible first."[4]

Daniel Martin was, we are told, a promising playwright and is a successful—which is to say, wealthy and celebrated—screenwriter. He feels deep dissatisfaction, however, with both his life and career. In some degree this book is a record of bookishness and a self-reflexive artifact in the modern mode; it explores its own conception, in both meanings of the term. And in that sense the eponymous novel is a conventional *Bildungsroman;* it ends with a beginning, a coming into consciousness—though the child at book's end is a middle-aged man. Dan has returned to England to start fresh, anew. And there are many references (including a coy one to *The French Lieutenant's Woman*) to possible alternate endings, to the nature of the novel, to matters of technique. Indeed, the book begins with a dazzling display of technique and can be read as a primer for narrative strategies, chapter by opening chapter. Let me do so, briefly, here.

The first chapter, "The Harvest," pays sustained stylistic homage to Thomas Hardy, the patron saint of the Devon landscape into which Daniel Martin was born. The language of the whole is, consciously, traditionbound, full of local dialect and repeated action: men haying in a field. "The crackle of the stubble, the shock of the stood sheaves. The rattle of the reaper; the chatter of the mower blades, the windmill arms above them, Lewis's voice at the corners: hoy then, hoy'ee, Cap'n, back, back, back, whoy, whoy."[5]

This sense of timelessness obtains as seasonal recurrence; all is as it once was. We are invited early on, however, to read this flashback as an act of retrospective witness; we first see Daniel Martin as "a boy in his mid-teens, his clothes unsuited, a mere harvest helper: cotton trousers, an apple-green Aertex shirt, old gym-shoes."[6]

Then we are jolted out of pastoral and into particularity: the English countryside and World War II. A German fighter plane appears and "The long combe is flooded with the frantic approach, violent machinery at full stretch, screaming in an agony of vicious fear. The boy, who is already literary, knows he is about to die."[7]

The plane passes overhead and winnowing resumes. Rabbits flee from the cleared fields and are caught and killed. "He moves closer and stares down at the pile, a good twenty now. And his heart turns, some strange premonitory turn, a day when in an empty field he shall weep for this."[8] From the threatened civilians to the slaughtered rabbits, mortality has entered in and, with it, consciousness. In the final action of the chapter, the young man carves his name into a tree:

> Deep incisions in the bark. . . . Adieu, my boyhood and my dream.
> Close shot.
> *D.H.M.*
> And underneath: *21 Aug 42.*[9]

The structuring devices of the novel have been rapidly established. The author moves with impunity from third to first person ("Adieu, my boyhood and my dream"), from the cinematic to the literary mode. The visual effect is that of film: an overview and a tracking long shot. But the directions are verbal: "Down, half marked by leaves. Point of view of the hidden bird."[10] Authorial distance entails a prolepsis—a flashforward as well as a backward glance: "The sky's proleptic name was California: the imperial static blue of August."[11] California will, throughout, serve as the polar opposite of the English countryside. And much of what follows will be, in effect, a crossing of cultural borders, a filling in of blanks.

By the second chapter we're in a thoroughly contemporary world. Some thirty-five years have elapsed between "The Harvest" and "Games"—which describes the sophisticated present-tense back-and-forth of Daniel Martin, screenwriter, and Jenny McNeill, actress. (Fowles gives his chapters titles in the traditional manner of the nineteenth-century novelist, but they somehow also provide cinematic captions to the action staged.) These theatrical antagonists engage in a lover's quarrel in Los Angeles; much of the chapter transpires through dialogue and dispassionate descriptive prose—this too inflected by movie talk: "A flicker of lighter flame. On the glass of the window he catches her momentary face, the long hair, the amber shadows of the couch. A whiteness where the indigo kimono, unabashed, lies open. A nice angle; nicest because no lens, no stock, could ever get it. Mirrors. The dark room."[12] Jenny has been urging her "scenarist" to attempt another genre and to write a novel; she offers to help him with notes. He is irresolute, however, and resists until, in the final phrase of this chapter, "unbelievably, as in a fiction, the door in the wall opens."[13]

We enter the past of that open door in "The Woman in the Reeds," a chapter of third-person descriptive prose having to do with postwar Oxford and the discovery of a drowned body. (As long previous as 1964, Fowles published a short story by that title; amateurish, it nonetheless sets the same scene.) Chapter 4 presents "An Unbiased View," and deploys yet another point of view—the epistolary mode of Jenny McNeill. She writes to "you"—the absent Dan—but calls him "Mr. Wolfe." Chapter 5 returns us to the present action and "The Door." Dan's ex-wife calls from England and urges his return to Oxford to deal with that unfinished business of which the book consists. Then chapter 6, "Aftermath," returns us—via the past tense—to postwar Oxford and "The Woman in the Reeds."

What I called "a dazzling display of technique" may well appear, on first exposure, merely dizzying; it's hard for the reader to establish purchase amid such shifting modes. These opening chapters are each composed in a different voice and from a different narrative vantage; the book settles down as it continues, but each of these voices recurs. Others too; a later long chapter, "Phyllida," is a sustained romantic reconstruction of young love—the sort of erotic pastoral at which Fowles excels. When conjoined to the world-weary anomie of the successful author (who returns to buy the house in which his first inamorata had lived) there's a literally breathtaking range of rhetorics and points of view—various ways of saying and seeing. This accumulation of styles, moreover, does not feel fragmented or disjunct; prismatic, rather, so that we end with a sense of sustained *consideration*, a multidimensional view. These are strategies devoted to engendering "whole sight." What began with Thomas Hardy ends with the aged Rembrandt's all-embracing gaze.

An early poem by John Fowles deals with much the same sense of the past lost/regained.

THE EXPERIENCE (1961)

You go down the right turnings
just as it says in the guide,
and it isn't there.

You turn up at the right room
at the right time,
in the right month and moonlight;
and it isn't there.

You discover the right grove,
you stand about on damp leaves.
A man on a tractor passes
and thinks you are mad.

You have the paper and the time,
you have the lot,
and nothing comes.

And it comes
at the start of a busy day
as you shave in a hurry,
cog with no time.

The wind. And you stand,
blinded till you are not blind.[14]

Further, there's the daring of what I want to call symbolic structure—a set of governing metaphors, or what Gardner termed "symbolically charged realism." Consider, for instance, the trip down the Nile as an emblem of Empire: on board are Frenchmen, Americans, a learned German, the English, and East Europeans—all vying, as it were, for centrality. Parallel lines have been drawn. A century before, it would have been colonial hegemony they fought for; now the jockeying for position takes place on a tourist boat. There's a commercial resurrection of buried life in the raising of a temple that would otherwise have perished behind the Aswan Dam; there are fellahin lining the shore.

The "Drowned Girl" of chapter 3—that bloated body of the woman in the reeds—associates with Jane herself (who uncovered the corpse when young and who herself has been submerged, if only analogically, in middle age). For much of the book's action she seems both suppressed and repressed, more than half in love with easeful death. What we have at novel's end is therefore a literal rebirth, a coming back to life in the desert where, stripped of all pretension by the harsh imperatives of Krak des Chevaliers, Jane shudders back to Dan's embrace and buries her wedding ring. Her husband, a severe Oxford don, has died; she is nakedly free now to take, again, Dan's hand. There are references to Orpheus and Eurydice, the dangers of a backward glance, the love that lasts through underworlds; references too to Isis and Osiris—though the protagonist is less than heroic in *Daniel Martin*, and too must be renewed. All this seems emblematic in a way that outstrips summary; for a novelist less wholly in control of craft, such symbol-

ism could look forced and overobvious. Here it feels justified, earned.

Consider too Daniel's reconciliation with Jane's hospital-
ized husband, Anthony, and the latter's suicide. Daniel has
crossed the Atlantic—at Anthony's request—to forgive and
be forgiven; he should have married Jane, not Nell, and Anthony has come to understand this, as well as his own youthful role in the comedy of errors that engendered misalliance.
"It's much more a matter of engineering. Of correcting a design failure. A little revenge on Madame Sosostris. And her
wicked pack of cards," says Anthony.[15]

It's all very Eliotic and earnest, this notion of a design flaw
to be corrected. Later, in the same crucial scene, the dying
man declares, "I'm still defeated by the conundrum of God.
But I have the Devil clear."

"And what's he?"
   "Not seeing whole."[16]

Once Daniel has agreed to spend some time with Jane
again, her husband seals the compact by killing himself that
same night. Anthony will risk damnation; he is a practicing
Catholic, after all, and not likely to have taken suicide lightly;
it's a sin embraced. "That odd phrase of his, 'correcting a design failure,' returned with a ghastly and macabre irony."[17]
We are asked to believe, in effect, that a moral error can be
mortal, that a mistake of one's youth can only be redressed at
great subsequent cost. This is a highly romantic view of mat-
uration, of passion diminished but not denied, and when Dan
and Jane at novel's end stand together in the kitchen as an acknowledged couple, we feel what was wrong is made right.
Fowles weds, in short, the way of seeing of a romantic fable to
the worldview of the realistic novel; the resulting "whole" has
been composed of fragmentary-seeming but cohesive parts.

I do have reservations. The book could have used an editor,
or at least self-scrutiny; it's so devoted to the notion of

nineteenth-century amplitude that it endorses *longeurs*. Entire disquisitions on Gramsci and Marx and the conditions of
Hollywood and the television industry might with profit
have been reduced. When Fowles waxes grandiloquent on
"the sacred combe" and "*la bonne vaux,*" he writes as an es-
sayist, not a novelist. Less would have been more. Daniel
Martin and his author are obsessed with the constraints of
"Englishness," but their attempt to escape from or qualify
the Oxbridge way of thinking succeeds only part of the time.
"Right feeling" is a quality both Dan and "his ill-concealed
ghost" admire, but it edges up to snobbishness: "She might
hide and hide, speak in cipher, betray her true self, but she
was still capable of a tenacity of right-feeling—that
strangest of all instransigences, both humanity's trap and its
ultimate freedom."[18]

The "heavenly sisters"—Jane and Nell—are too patly
paralleled by a pair of decidedly earthbound sisters with
whom Daniel also sleeps. And Jane is so resolutely self-
controlled, so quashed of spontaneity and squashed in her
persona that the resurrection at book's end seems largely notional. Jenny McNeill, by contrast, is one of Fowles's true
temptresses—but this makes Daniel's rejection of her and
embrace of Jane seem somehow willed: a "design flaw" corrected rather than a human truth played out. When Jenny
writes of her departed lover, "He has a mistress. Her name is
Loss,"[19] she comes very close to the mark.

This mismatched pair—middle-aged Dan and youthful
Jenny—have to "book" their transatlantic calls. They worry over the time differential, the hour in London as opposed
to L.A., and this is one of the ways the novel feels dated;
they'd be using e-mail or cell phones today. Political references to Nixon and Beirut in its prebombed splendor do give
this the feel of a period piece; Dan is forever descrying the
difference between the prewar generation (those who came
of age during World War II) and those to whom it's a historical footnote at best. A secondary character is old enough
to have once met Lord Kitchener—the figure on whom
Daniel bases his script in progress. Nell's second husband

Andrew—a fop while at Oxford—assumes his place in the squirarchy and countryside with scarcely a pause in his stride. And everyone knows everyone, it seems: the upstairs lodger in young Dan's rooming house, where he and Jane make love, is the selfsame Barney with whom his daughter, long years later, is having an affair—and with whom Dan converses on a transcontinental flight.

To be fair, however, this sort of coincidence is both representative of an insular society and the very stuff of the *Bildungsroman*. Nor does it escape its creator's notice; at each stage of the pilgrimage JF can comment on DM's proclivities and failures as well as his achievements. It's all an inside joke. And everywhere, in a book about *process*, the reader can observe the writerly *result*; Fowles records at the story's close those turnings of the journey that make of its end a beginning. If all this seems self-evident as well as a touch tricky, that's the price one pays when conjoining the postmodern to the traditional mode; Fowles eats his cake and has it too, I think. He writes a scene in the realist's vein, makes it convincingly sequential and natural-seeming, then closes the chapter with "Cut."

For, finally, this novel stands as the portrait of an artist as a young, then middle-aged man. It's hard not to think of Fowles himself as "the ill-concealed ghost" in this description of the movie world, hard not to read as autobiography the love of nature, the return to England and home. The purposely blurred point of view, the crisscrossing of narrative and geographical borders all serve to bring our author stage center. Examples of this shift between first and third person abound. Here are three:

> "I think Dan might at some point during that happy month have confessed, but he had some buried terror as to how confession might then run on or he clung to his secrets. . . .
>
> "Though the 99-year lease I bought of the Notting Hill flat was probably the best business deal I ever did, unaided, in my life, Dan and Nell began having doubts as soon as they moved in. . . .

"I indulged Nell. I knew we were spending too much, but if it brought more peace at home I felt it was justifiable.

"Then something predictive: one noon down at the studio Andrea seemed depressed a little, Dan asked her why, and she said it was her birthday. . . . "[20]

It follows therefore that this conjoined first-and-third person can write his book while engaged in the described procedure of imagining it:

He began to see the ghost of a central character, a theme, of a thing in the mind that might once more make reality the metaphor and itself the reality. . . . Spending a page or two on it is not quite outraging verisimilitude, since that morning Dad did, for an hour . . . start assembling a few notes on why he should leave the sanctuary of a medium he knew for the mysteries and complexities of one he didn't.[21]

Again,

The tiny first seed of what this book is trying to be dropped into my mind that day: a longing for a medium that would tally better with this real structure of my racial being and mind . . . something dense, interweaving, treating time as horizontal, like a skyling: not cramped, linear and progressive.[22]

The chapter titled "In the Orchard of the Blessed" is perhaps the crucial one in terms of artistic credo; it states case and problem at length:

The obstacle was this: he was too fortunate, and this gave him . . . a feeling of inauthenticity, almost of impotence. . . .

In short, he felt himself, both artistically and really, in the age-old humanist trap: of being allowed (as by some unearned privilege) to enjoy life too much to make a convincing case for any real despair or dissatisfaction. . . . With all his comparative freedom, money, time to think? His agreeable (despite his present grumbling) work? All artistic making, however imperfect, however tainted by commerce, was contenting compared to the work most of the rest of the world was condemned to. Even as Dan walked, he knew himself, partly in the very act of walking and knowing . . . dense with forebodings of a rich and happy year ahead. It was as ludicrous as that: forebodings of an even greater happiness—as if he were condemned to comedy in an age without it . . . at least in its old, smiling, fundamentally optimistic form. He thought, for instance, revealing instance, how all through his writing life, both as a playwright and a scenarist, he had avoided the happy ending, as if it were somehow in bad taste. . . .

It was like some new version of the Midas touch, with despair taking the place of gold. This despair might sometimes spring from a genuine metaphysical pessimism, or guilt, or sympathy with the less fortunate. But far more often it came from a kind of statistical sensitivity (and so crossed a border into market research), since in a period of intense and universal increase in self-awareness, few could be happy with their lot.

The dooming, self-accusing artist thus became like an Irish keener, a paid exhibitor of token feeling, a mourner for the unmourning.

Fowles here describes, it seems to me, a prevailing paradox of the contemporary writer's task—or at least a paradox attaching to success. More and more at a remove from the "trouble" that engenders art (the checklist could read "penury, exile, loss, abuse, addiction, etc."), he or she must nonetheless pretend to that trouble in book after book. The rich man writes of poverty, the famous woman of obscurity—and less and less persuasively as wealth and fame accrete. Daniel Martin and his author attain a new solution to the riddle posed by privilege and a resolution that,

> though it may seem a supremely self-centred declaration . . .
> is in fact a supremely socialist one. That it would not be recognized as such by a nearly entire majority of contemporary

socialists is, or so he will come to think, a defect in contemporary socialism; not in his decision.

To hell with cultural fashion; to hell with élitist guilt; to
hell with existentialist nausea; and above all, to hell with the
imagined that does not say, not only in, but behind the images, the real.[23]

Some years ago my family and I spent a night in the town of
Lyme Regis. We were driving through the area and there was
a good hotel and it was growing dark. Next morning we went
walking—down to the picturesque harbor, the quay made famous by *The French Lieutenant's Woman* and, earlier, Jane
Austen. Then we browsed a bit through curio shops, map
shops, bookshops, and in one of these I asked a lady at the
counter if she happened to know of, or know, a local writer
called John Fowles. I was a writer too, I said, and didn't want
to bother him but did want to walk past his house. She said, of
course, of course she knew him: his garden was just up the hill.

My wife and I walked up the hill and came upon it, *la
bonne vaux*, the place of his chosen retreat. There was a gate,
an entrance drive, a stately small house visible and, in its
doorway, Fowles. He was bidding hello to a woman in a
raincoat and making her welcome within. We could, I suppose, have approached him; I could have said how much I
admire his work. But such invasive temerity seemed wrong,
too blithe by half, and *Daniel Martin* demonstrates how little
pleasure its protagonist takes in similar encounters. We held
our peace.

Down, half marked by leaves. Point of view of the hidden
bird.[24]

I cannot call it desolation; what we saw was clear enough.
But all the rest of that visit I found myself imagining what it
would have felt like to be in his actual presence, to be like
Dan in Kenwood, gazing up at mastery: whole sight.

Strange Type

The writer Malcolm Lowry—most celebrated for his novel, *Under the Volcano*—wrote poetry also for much of his life. His characteristic obsessions (with fire, firewater, water, woe) inhabit the poems as well as the prose. At times his verses read like sketches for scenes in the novel, often verbatim, a way of trying out a phrase and deciding which genre works best. The lyric impulse, the formal rhetoric, the pleasure in word play: all these are vintage Lowry and survive the shift to rhyme. Here is the final entry in his *Selected Poems*, "Strange Type."

> I wrote: in the dark cavern of our birth.
> The printer had it tavern, which seems better:
> But herein lies the subject of our mirth,
> Since on the next page death appears as dearth.
> So it may be that God's word was distraction,
> Which to our strange type appears destruction,
> Which is bitter.[1]

For years I thought of this poem as quaint, a report on the printer's devil and antiquated technology: some thick-fingered transposition of letters while the type was being set.

My high school had a printing press, and I remember setting *m*s and *n*s: the hot metal shavings and protracted fumbling and my snail-paced progress toward a justified line. Each word was a procedure, every paragraph a trial. . . .

Yet anyone who reads today knows the "typo" is scarcely a thing of the past; error attends our new technologies as well. As Chair of the Hopwood Awards Committee at the University of Michigan, I recently proofread a volume—the fifth in a series—of lectures on "The Writing Life." Each April a prominent author delivers a speech to an audience of students, many of whom have been selected as recipients of a Hopwood Award; this "Advice to the Young Writer" is thereafter published in the *Michigan Quarterly Review*. That magazine is meticulous and the lectures appear letter-perfect, having been proofread repeatedly; once a sufficient number of such talks have been given and printed, I collect them and call it a book. The task of editing these pages should therefore be a simple one: gather the offprints together, scan them, and—hey presto!—a volume appears. . . .

Except it's not so simple and the scanning's inexact. There's an electronic imp at work with as much inventiveness as Lowry's comic printer—who substituted "tavern" for "cavern," "dearth" for "death." In the page proofs I corrected, for example, Robert Hass speaks of "the Creek tragedies" and Roger Rosenblatt of that contemporary American classic, *The Class Menagerie*. "Cod" is routinely invoked as our nation's deity, and one lecture was delivered by our present poet laureate Louise Cluck. These are, as it were, unhappy or *unglücklich* transpositions of Gluck and the rest, but the errata are not limited to a simple substitution of the letter *C* for *G*. The novelist DOS Passos looks like a tip of the typographer's cap to Microsoft, and there's the poet Alien Ginsberg—who might perhaps have welcomed his new name. One writer was "bounded from town to town," and there are whole lines revised at seeming-random. The machine has a will of its own.

I don't mean to complain, Luddite-like, about the failure of technology or to propose a return to the hand-set or handwritten page. But the proofreader's problem does point to a crucial disjunction—the distinction, as it were, between what we imagine and what we produce, the distance between reach and grasp. This may be a function of the eye and not the ear; as our sight dims and focus grows fuzzy, we tend to respond more to sound. The letters themselves can grow blurred. That proud Shakespearean boast, "So long as men can breathe and eyes can see/so long lives this, and this gives life to thee" carries a hint of its own countervailing assertion: men breathe and see but briefly, after all. One could almost read the vaunt as a form of *carpe diem*, for beauty too must fade. A writer cannot by definition predict what will outlast the act of writing or what it will signify in time to come; the work we envision and that we accomplish lie antipodes apart.

The preceding sentence or this one with which I now discuss it might prove resonant to others; more probably it won't. Yet its author cannot be the best judge or witness; the effect we have on readers is for readers to decide. If instead of "antipodes" I'd written "poles," and if that word were printed as "polls" or "Poles," there'd be a single letter's alteration but substantial change. From "distraction" to "destruction" is but a vocalic shift, and what a writer means or moans is hard to wean from mien. Atrocious as might seem this series of puns, it's Lowry-like and characteristic: or, as he put it in a letter to a friend, the sort of cartoonish "Tooloose Lowry-trek" that marked his rambling progress through typologies of text.

Too, he appeared to understand how his "volcano" would erupt. After years of poverty and failure, he earned great praise for his great book and, in "After Publication of *Under the Volcano*," wrote, "Success is like some horrible disaster/Worse than your house burning."[2] Much of what ensued were "the sounds of ruination"—another phrase from that poem—and when he died choking in drunken drugged sleep in a cottage in Ripe, Sussex in 1957, the coroner's verdict was "death by misadventure." One more couplet from his *Selected Poems*, and the unquiet Malcolm Lowry can rest a while in peace: "When the doomed are most eloquent in their sinking/It seems that then we are least strong to save. . . ."[3]

. . . .

Much has been made of the prose style of another prodigious drinker, Ernest Hemingway. His fame as artist will finally rest on stylistic innovation and not the characters or plot lines in his books. That stripped and luminescent thing, that eighth of an iceberg and "built-in-shockproof shit detector"—the plainspeak and colloquial diction so artfully wrought and architected—did more to change the look and sound of American prose than any other author's "in our time." (His phrase too. . . .) But the "eloquence" and "sinking" here seem part and parcel of the same phrase, two sides of the one coin.

Were a computer to dissect the patterns and the rhythm of Hemingway's language, it would, I'd guess, fail to distinguish between the early work and late—rather the way that the spellcheck can't distinguish between two proper English spellings, "there" and "their" or "weight" and "wait," that carry different meanings. Whatever failed him in the end was not the style itself.

For once he'd established his manner of expression, it more or less held fast. The Anglo-Saxon verbal pool in which he principally fished, the preponderance of monosyllabic if not four-letter words, the transliterated foreign speech and carefully buttressed abstractions, the spaced repetitions and lack of ascription in dialogue, the fondness for the present participle and paratactic use of the conjunction—all these are as present in his last pages as in his first. Some writers alter their style over time; think of William Butler Yeats, for example, or James Joyce. Or the early Henry James growing ever more grandiloquent and orotund, enlarging as his waistline did to the plump and jam-packed late. . . .

But others, once they forge a mode of discourse, hone and refine and retain it, and this is certainly the case with Hemingway; no other author I can think of was more constant, *consistent* in usage, less subject to change over time. Which is one of the reasons he's so simple to parody and why, in his worst work, he seems a shambling and parodic caricature of himself. So what's truly at stake here is substance not style;

this is the real distinction, the matter of the manner—what the French call *fond*, not *forme*. It's the difference, in effect, between the *cri du coeur* of Roland's horn and the empty honking of a boy who cries wolf, wolf. . . .

All this proves devastatingly applicable to the writer's final maunderings: the "novel"—the word requires quotes—*True at First Light*. The most recent (and, we are promised, the last) of his posthumously available books, it undermines the very structure it had been supposed to shore up. I mean by this the structure of published achievement, that imposing edifice which began in 1923 with *Three Stories and 10 Poems*. By now Hemingway has managed to produce nearly as much postmortem as during his productive career: *A Moveable Feast, Selected Letters, Islands in the Stream, The Garden of Eden,* and *True at First Light*—several thousand pages of prose have made their printed debut since he killed himself in 1961. And if you add, as his publishers do, the collections and selections—"That Dangerous Spring, That Dangerous Summer, That Dangerous Fall, That Dangerous Winter"—the list of Hemingway's titles at present available includes more that appeared *after* death than he chose while living to print.

Of these books, only the nearly completed first can lay proper claim to attention. Both forward-facing and elegiac, "the Paris stuff"—as Hemingway called it—adds to the bitter best we have of him and rounds the portrait out. But of the others, those hundreds and hundreds of pages accreted since his suicide, there's scant good news to report. Joan Didion, in a *New Yorker* article called "Last Words," makes a convincing case that these novels are not actual Hemingway but rather objects of commerce, leading inexorably to such things as the "Ernest Hemingway Collection" in furniture. Such commodification of an author's language has more to do with revenue than art; it's clear as can be that he wanted no part of this sort of publication and did try to cover his tracks. To have the last word is one of the dreams of a life committed to letters, and to have others decide how your finished text should read is a writer's nightmare brought to book.

This is a complicated issue, however, and best judged case by case. Those who read Franz Kafka must be grateful that Max Brod, his executor, disregarded his instruction that the work be burned. Virgil's *Aeneid* would have been unavailable, but so would a gaggle of second-rate efforts, the halt and unfinished and lame. Malcolm Lowry's fine collection of short fiction, *Hear Us O Lord from Heaven Thy Dwelling Place*, was published posthumously, as were those *Selected Poems* with which this essay begins. But the spate of subsequent books (*October Ferry to Gabriola*, *Dark as the Grave Wherein My Friend Is Laid*, etc.) have done little to advance his reputation. I myself, as John Gardner's literary executor, supervised the publication of two texts he left behind: one novel, *Stillness*, that he chose not to publish but his heirs approved of and one, *Shadows*, on which he was working at the time of his motorcycle accident. So I'm more than glancingly familiar with the difficulties of such an enterprise. Discretion seems the better part of valor, and one must navigate the minefields of early and discarded drafts with care.

Yet Hemingway did write Charles Scribner, in 1951, that certain parts of a long, four-part novel could be published intact after his death. In the ensuing decade he neither enjoined publication nor destroyed these manuscripts; he *could* have burned them, surely, or have left explicit instructions that the vault stay sealed. *The Old Man and the Sea*, indeed, is a self-contained part of that imagined whole; his readership is grateful it exists. And he himself oversaw the production of *Across the River and Into the Trees*, as bad a book as any that have been printed since his death. In 1929 he wrote, "There were many words that you could not stand to hear and finally only the names of places had dignity."[4] This passage from *A Farewell to Arms* poses the problem vividly: which words retain their dignity and which are better left unwritten, or at least unread?

I had been having chest pains for some weeks and maybe months. Like a stoical fool I ignored them, and they did go

away. At times the feeling in my chest seemed like acid re-
flux or a pulled muscle or—when in early May my wife and
I went walking in Bryce Canyon—discomfort from high al-
titude; at times it seemed like a result of dietary change.
Once or twice the pain stopped me in my tracks, but then it
dissipated—the taste of brass in my mouth fading, the ache
at my armpits released. In retrospect, of course, I know how
long and stupidly I ignored the warning signs, but nothing
had prepared me for *angina pectoris;* heart trouble happens to
others, and most of the time I felt fine.

For the last dozen summers I've spent a week or two with
friends in Saratoga Springs, New York. Robert and Peggy
Boyers began the New York State Summer Writers' Institute as a close approximation of and successor to the Bennington Writing Workshops, of which I had been Founding
Director a quarter of a century ago. William and Dana
Kennedy established something similar in Albany, and its
summer outpost, the writing workshop in Saratoga, starts at
June's end. It felt and feels important to remain in touch with
the Kennedys, the Boyers, and Marc Woodworth and Emma
Dodge Hanson, who live off the edge of the Skidmore College campus and constitute a kind of writing family. Frank
Bidart, Carolyn Forché, and Mary Gordon are a part of that
faculty also; Richard Howard, Robert Pinsky, and a host of
others come to campus year after year. There are old haunts
to revisit: cafés and restaurants to gather in and, in the mornings, breakfast at the practice sessions at the track. . . .

Elena and I drove east from Ann Arbor; then, having
spent a day at Skidmore, she drove on. Her parents live on
outer Cape Cod, and it had been months since she'd seen
them, so I occupied our rooms alone and settled down in the
high heat to teach. There was a good deal to do. I had a set
of manuscripts to critique, students to confer with, and
workshops to conduct. On Tuesday night of that first week
I gave a reading, together with Francine Prose, of our novels in progress; the audience seemed to approve. Russell
Banks came by and we went out drinking till midnight or so,
delighted to catch up. Russ had just returned from Sierra

Leone, and he was full of stories of the horror and excitement of it, and when we parted we embraced. I remember him saying, "Look at us, we're both in good health and lucky, very lucky." What could I do but agree?

The next afternoon I taught a three-hour "Advanced Prose Fiction" workshop; then Michael Ondaatje arrived for his scheduled performance that night. This all sounds, I'm aware, like literary name-dropping, a parlor game, but it's the great gift of the New York State Summer Writers' Institute to make an extended family of those who come to town. We had dinner together beforehand; a dozen or so friends at table— much laughter and many bad jokes. I was to introduce Ondaatje and had prepared my words with care; Michael's off-hand and informal public manner cannot disguise the rigor of his close attention or veil his gimlet gaze. I gave my speech; he gave his reading; there was thunderous applause. Many plaudits; mutual congratulations; all was well. . . .

Which is not the whole story, of course. There are other things to say. From the moment that Elena left and I commenced to walk the campus—we had used a car before—the pain in my chest had increased. The days were hot, but I was sweating even after fifty feet; the taste in my mouth was of tin, then brass, the ache in my chest enlarging. On Tuesday the mere act of walking began to seem quite difficult; on Wednesday I had to pause for breath each twenty uphill yards, and a flight of stairs looked Everest-like. I could no longer pretend to be fine and sent an e-mail to my elder brother Thomas—a doctor at Harvard Medical School— asking what was wrong.

He told me, not mincing words, that what I described was serious and not mere indigestion. "It's called unstable angina, crescendo angina," Tom said, "and don't let them give you a stress test because you'll no doubt fail." I reached my doctor in Ann Arbor; he said—even more bluntly—the same. My brother called in a prescription for nitroglycerine tablets to the local pharmacy and said, "The next time that you feel the pain take one of those, and if the pain does go away then don't pass go, go to the emergency room." After dinner with Ondaatje I had indeed had trouble walking to the hall where we spoke, and I did take a tablet and the pain did go away. When the reading was over, therefore, I asked my friends if they would take me to the Saratoga Hospital emergency room. Mary Gordon was to read next night, and as we left I told her I might have to miss the occasion and, in advance, apologized. The shocked look on her face informed me—as nothing else that week had done—how much I'd risked for the *beau geste*, how reckless my stiff-upper-lippish sticking to the program could in fact have been. . . .

Emma Dodge Hanson drove me to the hospital. She's a spectacular-looking creature, six feet tall and with a high whinnying laugh that both attests to and engenders pleasure in the world. That night she did not laugh. Instead Emma saw me through the process of admission and the first medical inquiries: Was I nauseated? Was I sweating? Were there shooting sensations in my feet and arms? Cell phones are not permitted near the hospital's machinery, and every few minutes she would withdraw to call her husband or Bob Boyers and report on what seemed like progress: I had been stabilized and was no longer in pain. After some time and at my urging, Emma left, and—hooked up now to oxygen and heparin to thin the blood—I lay back and tried to take stock.

That was the soul's dark night for me—the hours on a gurney while the emergency room filled and emptied and the personnel changed shifts. I had never before spent a night in any sort of hospital, and this one was far from home. The machinery bleeped noisily and nurses shuttled past me and I wanted to go to the bathroom but was attached to tubes; I missed my wife, our daughters, my sense of self and privacy, my recent heedless health. "*Lente, lente, currite noctis equi,*" cries Marlowe's Faust near the end of *Doctor Faustus*, but my own nightmares ran swiftly; what had I done or left undone to end up in this place?

A cardiologist appeared; he assured me that I was stabilized and said they could perform an angiogram but not the invasive procedure of an angioplasty, and therefore would send me to Albany or, if I preferred it, somewhere else. "There's a first-rate facility at Cooperstown," he said, "and afterward you might want to pay a visit to the Baseball Hall of Fame." My brother worked and taught, I told him, at the Beth Israel–Deaconess Medical Center in Boston, and they were ready to admit me. "That's fine," he said, "that makes good sense," and he was going home because he'd come to work at eight o'clock that day and it was nearly midnight and his shift was over now, and he wished me well and patted my arm and withdrew. . . .

The horses of the night stopped galloping and slowed to a canter, then a trot; two o'clock gave way to four and four o'clock to six. I could not see the dawn but knew it had arrived. The other patients in the emergency room—white-haired old women, a one-legged man, a girl with tattoos riding up past her jeans—came, went, and were admitted to the hospital or treated and released. In the early morning Marc Woodworth appeared to tell me that Elena and our younger daughter Andrea were driving over from Cape Cod.

Then Bill and Dana Kennedy and Michael Ondaatje and Linda Spaulding came through the doors with coffee and the *New York Times*, and though the nurses shooed them out again, I had a paper cup and newspaper to attest to friendship and their collective concern. By the time my family arrived, I felt ready to drive off with them; this was A.M.A., the administrator said—"against medical advice." If I wanted to risk it, it wasn't their fault, but since we had a cell phone and there were hospitals along the way, and if my wife was willing to accept responsibility and to do the driving, we could leave.

I signed a piece of paper that acknowledged this, absolving them, and dressed. In that little cubicle, however, I felt the band of pain again—the taste of brass back in my mouth. It was anxiety, no doubt, but sharp enough to register; we decided to follow the doctor's advice and be less sorry than safe. Elena and Andrea left once more, making their weary way to Boston and a hotel near the hospital; I spent that afternoon and evening waiting for the ambulance to come.

On the trip from Saratoga Springs I lay on my back, facing out the window. I have made that drive often and know the road well, but the shift in perspective does change what you see: the blank side of road signs, the play of the clouds. It grew dark. We took the Northway south and then the turnpike east. A man called Jim drove and a man called Henry sat with me; he strapped me in and then kept checking my blood pressure and temperature and pulse. He offered oxygen; I said I thought I didn't need it and was happy to lie down and rest.

My attendant was gentle, affable, and seemed to want to talk. He spoke about his children—a teenaged son who was no trouble and a daughter who very much was—and the breakup of his marriage and the courses he had taken to qualify as a PA (physician's assistant); he saw I was reading Noel Coward—*Private Lives*, *Blithe Spirit*—and told me he himself had just read *Zorba the Greek* and *The Last Temptation of Christ*. For years Henry had operated a stationery store; it was steady work but not rewarding and he meant this, he explained, not in the pecuniary sense.

That was his word—"pecuniary"—and the rest of his diction was formal as well. He framed each sentence with care. He had met a man, he told me, who translated Kazantzakis and thought Nikos Kazantzakis was an excellent writer who very much merited attention. We agreed. Henry worked long hours three days a week and, on a night like this one, would sleep on a cot in the office and take a shower there when they returned from Boston; I apologized for taking him away from home and a chance to wake up on the Fourth of July weekend at his own place with his two children, and he said—again his words—that I should not concern myself with "his itinerary or emoluments"; it was his job.

At Beth Israel–Deaconess Medical Center, they were expecting us. There was paperwork to do: insurance forms and questionnaires and privacy release forms and declarations to sign. I answered the by now familiar litany of questions and had my blood extracted and my pulse checked and my temperature and blood pressure taken and sat through an EKG. There was a room upstairs, they told me, where I would go once admitted, but there were admissions procedures, and the procedures take time. Time slows in the hospital, shifting its gears; the next night, for example, I would be awakened at 11:15, at 1:30, at 3:15 and 5:15 by personnel who wanted to assure themselves I slept.

Three days went by. I met a dozen doctors and a dozen residents and interns and medical fellows and technicians and nurses on rotation; I watched *Breakfast at Wimbledon*—the semifinals and the final tennis matches—and tried to write and read. On weekends and holidays the hospital restricts itself to emergency procedures, the unexpected arrival by ambulance or helicopter, and I no longer qualified. There was nothing to do now but wait. The medical team assured me that, if I had a heart attack, they'd deal with it immediately, but otherwise I'd have to be—the attending physician made a joke—a patient patient until Monday morning, when they would be full-staffed. This made a kind of administrative sense, and I tried to stop complaining, but by my fifth night in a hospital I was growing querulous; bed rest and "heart-healthy" food took their toll, and I was beginning to wonder if indeed I'd ever needed medical attention, or if instead I should have let the problem take care of itself.

"Is it possible," I asked the young men and women who listened to my heart and lungs, "there's simply nothing wrong?"

"It's possible," they said.

On Monday morning, however, reality set in. I was scheduled for the first procedure—a reward for my three-day delay—and transferred to a gurney and trundled to the "prep" room, where a dozen lean and fresh-scrubbed men and women hurried past. They looked like dancers, joggers, with a poised balls-of-the-feet forward motion that made everything seem urgent; they were wearing sneakers, jocular, catching up on the weekend and who had done what and gone where. It was as though they'd prepped for work by watching reruns of *ER*.

I answered the questions—Any pain? Any nausea? Any allergies to medication?—again. I had my blood pressure and temperature checked, a final EKG performed; I was shaved on both sides of the groin ("They like to go in from the right side," said the nurse—electric razor in her hand—"but if for some reason they need to go left, we need to shave that side too"). She was sunburned from the rooftop where she had watched the July 4 fireworks, and I spent some time attempting to make sense of this. How would you get a sunburn at night? Don't they set off the fireworks at night? Then she explained that she'd been on the rooftop that afternoon also, and I understood the Valium they'd given me was working; by the time she produced a "condom catheter" and told me I might need to urinate during the procedure—it would take an hour, maybe two—I smiled and affixed it, stopped trying to chat.

Then again the trip down corridors and through metal sliding doors to the "state-of-the-art" operating theater, the easy intimacy with men and women I had never seen before and would not again. My brother's name had currency here; they worked with him, had been hired or taught or supervised by him, and they chatted amiably about the family and the weather while I tried to stay coherent and shake hands. An angiogram is simple enough, an increasingly common procedure, and the "interventional cardiologist" who performed it had a kind of practiced patter—"This is the worst part, this is where you'll feel a little pinprick. You can watch the screen if you want to, we're going up through the groin." Then he told me that the dye they were injecting would feel warm, would maybe sting a little; they were taking pictures and tracking the way my arteries looked. Then I was no longer his anticipated audience but an object of instruction while he lectured the young doctors at his side.

There was a flurry of controlled activity, a series of maneuvers; I could watch them working and they looked like pinball players, hands manipulating instruments beneath my line of sight. I never did lose consciousness; I watched the screen and clock, or tried to; I told the nurse each time she asked that yes, I was feeling just fine. But something in the surgeon's voice had warned me I was becoming "interesting"—dread word in the medical lexicon—and was no longer routine.

When he told me, at procedure's end, what they'd done and not done, I recognized how close I'd come to death. Or, as the doctor preferred to put it, "a major coronary incident," a myocardial infarction that would have done substantial damage to the heart. One of my arteries was fine, he said, and one completely blocked. This had happened—it was hard to say precisely when—some years before. But the body has its way of dealing with such blockage; you can have a heart attack and think it's indigestion and never really notice that the blood supply's hunting an alternate route through the delta of your chest; the phrase is "collateral" establishment but it's the good kind of collateral, not what they're finding nowadays as damage in Iraq. My doctor smiled. "You're the language man here," he declared. "In any case, there's nothing we can do about that network of collateral veins" and, in effect, they're okay. "They've performed their own bypass," he said.

"It's the main artery that was giving you the trouble: the LAD—left anterior descending—was 90 percent occluded. Let me show you the pictures, okay?" He gave a technician a series of numbers, and on the screen at my side an image appeared: gray-blue, webbed with a network of lines. There was a narrowing, an evanescence, a place where the blood failed to course. "*This* is what it looked like," said the surgeon, "and *this* is what it looks like now; we inserted, as I said we would, a stent. It's kind of like a hose," he said, "and the stent is mesh inside your artery to keep it from narrowing down. Here's a before-and-after photograph; put it on your refrigerator door at home and stay away from cheese. And you've had your last drink of buttermilk and your final piece of steak. Consider yourself very lucky it's not six months ago, because there's a new kind of stent—they've had it in Europe," he said ruefully, "for *years* but we only just got clearance—which is coated with a kind of antistick. You can think of it as Teflon though it's really a kind of repellent, so platelets won't gather there and, after a period, clot. These are state of the art, in short supply. The perfect fit would have been 13 millimeters but we only had a CYPHER stent that's the right width and 23 millimeters long; much of what was going on was how I adjusted the length. That's why they sent you here," he said. "Time was there would have been two separate procedures—one a diagnosis, one an intervention—but we prefer combining them and give you two for one."

The cardiologist talked on and on in this fashion while I faded in and faded out and tried to pay attention; what it came down to, he repeated, was that I had waited far too long but caught it just in time. "You'll be on medication now, you'll pay more attention, and we'll have to monitor against stenosis—the body might try to reject what we've done—but if the recovery goes according to schedule, you can go home tomorrow."

It did; we were released. Friends came to the hospital room, bearing flowers and champagne. We drank the latter, left the former at the nurses' station, and decamped. I grew newly familiar with medical terms, the cluster of invented words—part Latin, part Greek, mostly Drugspeak—that would constitute henceforth a part of my vocabulary and indenture me to pharmacists. I would drop multicolored capsules into a plastic container with seven compartments for days of the week; I would substitute red wine for white and take a daily dose of folic acid and Omega-3 fish oils. I would learn to use words like "hemodynamics" and "cardiac/peripheral catheterization" and "electrophysiology"; I would try to make some sense of "interventional details" such as the following: "We then crossed into D1 with PT graphix wire and performed kissing balloon inflations with 3.0 x 15 balloon in LAD and 2.5 x 15 balloon in DI."

I had dodged a rather large and not-so-silver bullet; the doctors were pleased with themselves. In the "Assessment & Recommendations" section of the report they sent me home with, the first item was "Successful PCI of culprit LAD/D1 lesion." The "culprit . . . lesion" had been dispensed with; there was instead a "Brisk flow." In this new-minted language set, a phrase like "kissing balloons" or "culprit lesion" had its own intrinsic poetry, and the data's metric pattern seemed possible to scan. . . .

"We're getting better all the time at managing the heart," my brother said. "Ten years ago there was just a balloon and ten years from now I'm guessing we'll get rid of plaque by pills. If you have to have a major organ that's in trouble, let it be the heart. We're not as good repairing lungs and livers yet, or brains. And though the system's in crisis, though everyone complains about the medical establishment, it's better to be sick today than ever before in our history; thank your lucky stars this happened in America, and now. . . ."

Elena took the wheel. She'd logged two thousand miles since, ten days earlier, we'd left our home in Michigan for what had been supposed to be an easy ramble east; I wasn't permitted to drive. We spent the night in Geneva, New York, on the north shore of Lake Seneca. I had been there years before, giving a talk at Hobart & William Smith Colleges, and had a happy if vague recollection of the place; the Finger Lakes region is peaceful, and its wines are good. The small town of Geneva is the place where Dr. Dick Diver—at the end of F. Scott Fitzgerald's *Tender Is the Night*—rusticates and charms the ladies; too, it marks the halfway point from Boston to Ann Arbor. In all our previous such trips, we'd driven the whole distance, setting out in predawn dark and spelling each other at the wheel and arriving home by nightfall; now the journey seemed too long to make in a single day.

When we checked into a lakeside inn, Elena carried our luggage; I tottered along behind. No doubt there had been fireworks on Independence Day; no doubt the lake could be wind-whipped and threatful, but everything seemed placid at this outer edge of town. The early summer evening was warm and clear and windless; we took "a constitutional" on the boardwalk by the shore. Music crept by us on the water, and we made our slow way to its source. The Finger Lakes Symphony Orchestra was entertaining citizens with a concert from a bandstand; they were performing a medley from *Oklahoma* while families were picnicking and reading newspapers and, sprawled in lawn chairs, gorging on Big Macs. Everywhere I noticed—newly conscious of the plague of it—the size of their stomachs, the heft of their thighs, and though I'm far from underweight, I felt unfairly singled out: *my* stomach didn't spill over its belt, *my* legs had muscles in them, so why should *I* have been weighed in the balance and found wanting? What moving finger pointed at me; why?

This is a common reaction in patients, a reflexive self-defense. In the ledger charting such statistics we read only "I, I, I." There's no history of heart disease in my long-lived family; my cholesterol was elevated but not enough to alarm my physician, and the "good" cholesterol level was high. Thirty years ago I affected a pipe but never cigarettes; I did not smoke. The only medicine I took was aspirin, the only time I saw a doctor was for an annual check-up and he told me, always, smiling, to come back at the same time next year. On the checklist for risk factors I checked none. Yet my arteries paid no attention to this self-satisfied assessment and a piece of plaque in a location that my brother called "the widowmaker" nearly did me in. . . .

"Pore Judd is daid," the brass section brayed, and we returned to the hotel. The jetty seemed endless, expansive; I measured my steps to its end. Children were eating popcorn and ice cream and French fries and hot dogs and drinking great vats of sweet drinks. We drove through town and found a small Italian trattoria and settled in its outdoor "dining space"—a porch festooned with painted vines and plastic grapes and loudspeakers offering songs in Italian— "Volare" and "Arrividerci, Roma," and sobbing treacly solos by Julias La Rosa and Mario Lanza and Vic Damone. We ate fish.

I have written this as retrospect, and in the past tense. It is an ongoing story, of course, and one that I hope will be long. Too, it's a common narrative; almost every adult in America—and certainly every middle-aged man—is at risk of heart disease, a hardening of the arteries; what I went through is not even called an "operation," only a "procedure." Once the episode was over, I heard story after story of heart bypasses, heart transplants, of open-heart surgery and angioplasties performed years ago: damage that beggared my own. As a cautionary tale, this offers no real moral. But nonetheless and in the watches of the night, I see myself on that hospital gurney or in the dark ambulance or lying on the table while the doctors focus on the screen that shows my heart and blood, and while those brood mares thunder past, I remember Faust's hard bargain and his fear as the chimes chimed. He was quoting Ovid, who in his *Amores* petitioned a long evening's pleasure and who equally had to submit to the clock. The horses of the night run slowly, slowly, but they continue to run. . . .

It sometimes seems as though F. Scott Fitzgerald and Ernest Hemingway invented the concept of author as public figure and grist to the media mill. (They didn't, in truth; Ralph Waldo Emerson made his living on the circuit, and Mark Twain and Charles Dickens were modern celebrities equally: half artist, half entertainer to those who came to hear them in the lecture halls. Walt Whitman, Carl Sandburg, Oscar Wilde—the list extends, expands. But the divide between life and letters, between the performer and the thing performed, appears in all those other instances more clear.) Fitzgerald at career's end worked in near-anonymity and with great integrity; not so the man who'd mocked him as "poor Scott." Dickens or Twain may have drawn on per-

sonal history for the characters of David Copperfield or
Tom Sawyer, but no one who thronged to listen thought of
their fictions as fact. That distinction has been—in no small
part because of Hemingway—erased. When he writes
about his hero's war service or guerrillas in the Spanish hills
or hunting German submarines, we tend to take the imagined tale—no matter how wild and self-serving—for the
enacted deed.

This no doubt fuels the pointless argument that *True at
First Light* has engendered: the question of whether or not he
took an African bride. The protagonist of that novel in
progress is offered a willing maiden or two, and it titillates
the imagination to think its author was too. Hemingway
claimed to have slept with Mata Hari—a chronological im-
possibility—and his rum-bred braggadocio as to Dietrich,
Garbo, and the rest seems interestingly at odds with his character's earned reticence. If he's correct in his assertion that
you lose it if you talk about it, then he lost in actuality what
on the page he gained.

It's one paradox of our age of publicity that authors such
as J. D. Salinger and Cormac McCarthy and Thomas Pyn-
chon can increase their public's expectation by the very re-
fusal to appear on talk shows or in Dewar's ads; were they to
show up at fashion shoots, we'd be less likely to look for the
texts. It's a ploy of publicity agents now to keep their clients
under wraps and a book's contents sealed. But this of course
requires that someone *notices* your absence from the limelight; most of us don't need to be protected from the pa-
parazzi's flash. For me to refuse Oprah Winfrey's invitation
to appear on her television program is somewhat less heroic
than it would be if she asked. In this sense the "author tour"
represents its own contradiction; to write your name in lights
or at the bookstore table is not to be at home alone engendering the work. What we lose in the process is that most
cherished aspect of the writer's life, untrammeled time to
work. And Hemingway did understand this; he was, it would
seem, a binge writer—alternating periods of privacy with
those of the fiesta (which is, as it happens, the German title

of that book of his which in English alludes to the fact of recurrence and the vanity of worldly hope: the sun also riseth
until, one day, it sets). His biographers' accounting of the
bleak final years attests to the writer's conviction that the act
of creation mattered, mattered greatly, and he killed himself
at least in part once he began to fear he could no longer write.

Here it's useful to remember how many of his heroes are
cognate figures for the artist: from Jake Barnes the journalist
to Thomas Hudson the painter, men of sensibility take stage
center in the tales. The great white hunter Robert Wilson, in
"The Short Happy Life of Francis Macomber," recites
Shakespeare on the subjects of bravery and growth. Even the
least literate of Hemingway's protagonists, the Cuban fisher-
man Santiago, responds to the water and sunset as though he
were composing the scene: *conscious* sensibility is a common
denominator throughout. This holds true for the *corrida* and
trout stream as well as the safari. His men may be silent and
stiff upper-lipped, but the dying Harry of "The Snows of
Kilimanjaro" provides the model here: writing what he cannot write in a kind of soundless cadenza and, in the form of
the hyena, giving concrete shape to death.

Too, it's startling to remember how young our author was
when first famous; most of his time was lived in the limelight,
and even the retreats—Key West, the African rambles—
were open to photographers. This writer's life was relent-
lessly public, fully exposed from "first light." Fitzgerald
wrote the editor Maxwell Perkins in 1924: "This is to tell you
about a young man named Ernest Hemingway, who lives in
Paris (an American), writes for the transatlantic review and
has a brilliant future. I'd look him up right away. He's the
real thing." At this point "Hem" was not yet twenty-five, so
the apprenticeship was at best brief. Now we'd announce
"the arrival of a major new talent" and talk of movie rights
sales and TV interviews and blockbusting tours. But Hemingway was ballyhooed at least as early on in life as, say, Bret
Easton Ellis or Jay McInerney or Tama Janowitz.

To name this more or less contemporary trio is to recognize how rapidly today fame fleets. "The bubble reputation"

may remain as a function of name recognition but not artistic laurels; there will be a hundred now who know that these people are writers for every one who plans to read their books. Unmediated judgment attaches largely to an anonymous manuscript; from then on out it's a matter of gossip columns and sales. I mean by this that the first reader of the first submission must trust his or her own educated guess as to a manuscript's worth. Thereafter, other issues factor in. The commercial stakes have been raised; the tolerance for failure or a break-even book decreases, it would seem, each season. So the decision as to whether to publish the new Ellis, McInerney, or Janowitz, whether to review or read, has more to do with previous sales records than the intrinsic value of the text at hand. And I pick these three at near-random; for a whole raft of reasons, it's hard to extend a career.

Of all the second acts in American literary life, there's none more sad than Hemingway's, and it helps to be reminded of his brilliantly accomplished first. When Fitzgerald called himself "an indifferent caretaker . . . of talent," Hemingway was savage, saying of *The Crack-Up* that it was dirty laundry and should not be washed in public. But *True at First Light* paints a far grimmer picture—grim because involuntary as well as self-deluded—of an author gone bankrupt, or at least into receivership. For even in his wildest dreams the boy in Oak Park at the turn of the century could not have predicted that, by the millennium, there would be furniture marketed in his name and in four individually tailored themes: Ketchum, Key West, Havana, and Kenya. There are Hemingway look-alike contests, Hemingway write-alike contests, the bearded face licensed to T-shirts and soon enough, no doubt, to gin. What does all this have to do with writing, one may ask?

The germ of *Under the Volcano* lies in a short story, of the same name, written by Malcolm Lowry in Cuernavaca, Mexico, in 1936. That novel was published (with the short story enlarged and transformed into chapter 8) in 1947. Few books have been more carefully reworked. In its decade of gestation,

Under the Volcano grew from a diffuse, effusive embryo to an elaborate contrivance of a novel, its whole built of interlocked parts. Lowry, an amateur numerologist, created here a trochal "book of numbers," with twelve and seven at the turning points. The opening chapter, both introduction and coda, is the first of twelve and takes place a year after the action as such—appropriately enough, on "The Day of the Dead." The action itself lasts but a day, and is the single action of the hero's death.

This writer wrote all of his life. He was conscious of vocation early on, and self-conscious in the extreme; his first letter to a much-admired stranger, Conrad Aiken, begins: "I have lived only nineteen years and all of them more or less badly."[5] Like many a young author's, his apprentice novel was derivative; *Ultramarine* owes much to Aiken's own *Blue Voyage* and the work of Nordahl Grieg. By the time his masterpiece was fully fledged, however, Lowry's borrowings were not so much disguised as functional; *Under the Volcano* makes fruitful use of such antecedents as the Bible, *Don Quixote*, the Divine Comedy, *Hamlet*, and—germane in this case—Marlowe's *Faust*.

In the speech to which I've here referred, the doomed magician perorates:

> *O lente lente currite noctis equi*
> The stars move still, time runs, the clock will strike . . .
> Then will I headlong run into the earth
> Earth, gape! O no; it will not harbor me.[6]

In chapter 1 of the novel, Jacques Laruelle finds his old copy of the Modern Library edition of Elizabethan plays—a book he had given the dead Geoffrey Firmin—and, opening it at random, reads:

> Then will I headlong fly into the earth:
> Earth, gape! it will not harbour me![7]

At novel's end, more than three hundred pages later, this is precisely what has happened to the Consul; he has been shot and thrown into a ditch. Laruelle shuts the volume, shaken, and the long retrospect begins. It's a book filled with learned allusions, punning referents (the Consul calls a kitten "Oedi-pusspuss" and "catastrophe," not to mention "katabasis"), and pidgin English: "She is the Virgin for those that have no-body them with," or "Half past sick by the cock." But here is an example of that "strange type" Lowry found "bitter": the troubled Laruelle, who has been "least strong to save," mis-reads the lines from Marlowe and, by substituting "fly" for "run," performs a kind of editorial interpolation. His friend's remembered action suits the altered word.

Within the twelve hours of the last eleven chapters, and in conformity (as in Joyce's *Ulysses*) with strict chronological possibility, various freedoms are taken with time. The last two chapters are simultaneous; lengthy flashbacks flesh out the narrative, interior monologues interrupt dialogue, delir-ium works contrapuntal to urbane discussion. In the confu-sion and welter of events, people get lost in the dark wood and, tracking each other, diverge. Letters sent are never read; letters written, never sent. Appointments made are soon forgotten, Spanish signs are misunderstood or inaccu-rately translated, seeming speeches stay unvoiced. Dramatic tension in the book consists of the despairing and fore-doomed attempt of its characters to bridge distance; their tragedy is that of chances missed.

Yet deliberate reworking made of *Under the Volcano* a true tour de force; the possessed artist, by dint of tenacity, grew self-possessed. The accidents of geographical distance (he lived most of his productive life in Dollarton, British Co-lumbia) and literary exile may have helped. Like his Faust-ian protagonist, the writer struggled with demons, and the semisober years in Dollarton proved fruitful in the extreme. Lowry, uncertain five years after its inception and before the final draft, wrote, "It may be that the adverse conditions un-der which the book was finally written influenced me to think it was an artistic triumph when it was only a sort of moral one."[8] I believe it an instance of both.

In Defense of Quotation

In the course of this last year, and without conscious intention, I have been to places with matched names. My wife and I spent the month of March in the small resort town of Bellagio; in May and the large city of Las Vegas we went to the Bellagio Resort Hotel. Such a pairing is hard to ignore. The north of Italy and state of Nevada share no obvious relationship, but the noun "Bellagio" connects them each to each. The coordinates of a mind's map may be loose-edged and inexact, yet city fathers, city planners everywhere mark where their parents' parents came from when they begin to name names. . . .

Consider the map of New England. There's a Concord, Brewster, Plymouth, or Manchester in most of the northeastern states; they suggest a common ancestry or a tip of the traveler's cap. Those settlers who journeyed a hard month or year on their errands to the wilderness could not have dreamed how readily we'd compass, in this modern age, two or three cities with the identical name. The Arlington of Massachusetts—to take a near-random example—is but a morning's drive away from the Arlington in Vermont; Greenwich, Connecticut and Greenwich, New York sit four highway hours apart. The village due east of Greenwich,

New York, is called Cambridge; the town to the north is called Salem—in honor, I assume, of those towns in Massachusetts from which their "founding fathers" traveled west. South along New York's Route 22 lie the villages of Chatham and North Petersburg and New Lebanon; this kind of repetitive naming is not the exception but rule.

Place words that sound an echo seem neither a failure of imagination nor a result of the limits of nomenclature. Rather, they suggest the habit of quotation. There's more than one Hot Springs or Middletown because such titles are descriptive; the Lincolns and Washingtons and Monroes and Madisons in their several states refer to men honored and dead. Portland, Maine and Portland, Oregon are called the same because of functional geography; so too with the Springfields, Boulders, and Centervilles that dot our nation's map. But a sizable proportion of the city names of America have to do with simple retrospect; we memorialize where we came from when we start anew.

The idea of family seems relevant here also. Strasbourg and Osaka can turn up on the unlikeliest billboards as "sister cities" in a dream of global linkage; Ann Arbor, Michigan— for reasons best known to its chamber of commerce—has been paired with Tubingen, Germany and Hikone, Japan. Yet how does Paris, Texas relate to its original, or Ithaca and Troy, New York to the work of the blind bard? New Orleans derives from the Orleans in France, New York from the York of Great Britain in ways that seem self-evident, but which yearning for antiquity led the settlers of Athens, Georgia, or Athens, Ohio to endow their new-staked plots of land with that enduring name? What, if anything, do these places have in common? How do they refer to each other, and what might the referent mean?

Another way of looking at this has to do with painting. That great portrait by Manet which alludes to its great predecessor by Velázquez—two black-garbed men standing on air—is an act of reverence and a form of artistic quotation. Elsewhere I've argued that imitation is the essence of apprenticeship, and those who would acquire a craft must copy those who practiced it before. The way Goya studied Velázquez, however, and the way he was in turn reproduced by Manet has more to do with emulation than with slavish copying; in this regard, the process of quotation *must* be inexact. Brahms's "Variation on a Theme by Haydn" announces both indebtedness and independence; musicians everywhere refer—and the technical term *is* "quotation"—to music made elsewhere and previously. In the cultural transmission children take for granted—our parents' opinions codified or, turn by turn, resisted, our memories and anecdotes rehearsed in company once more—there's an element of variation but a constant theme. Look at the last sentence of this essay's opening paragraph ("parents' parents . . . name names") and note how a kind of repetition compulsion enters into syntax. If the child is father to the man, the reverse is also true; we are what we were and will be. . . .

The small town of Bellagio hugs the blue shore of Lake Como. It occupies the promontory that divides the two lower parts of that body of water; the lake extends thereafter to the north. In wintertime the resort shuts down; the hotels and restaurants and shops that welcome tourists all close for renovation; the cobbled streets are torn apart, the water mains repaired. I have been there in the summer, when the narrow steep-pitched alleys are full of camera-toting and ice cream–eating visitors; by contrast, in the month of March the buildings and their gardens are "*Chiuso,*" undisturbed.

The Villa Serbelloni dominates the town's green crest. Owned since 1959 by the Rockefeller Foundation, it boasts a storied past. Pliny the Younger called the grounds home, and Roman roof tiles have been unearthed from beneath the grass of the terraces; smaller renovated buildings climb the stages of the hill. Leonardo may have mapped a stream nearby. Stendahl set *The Charterhouse of Parma* in the region, and *I Promessi Sposi* starts with a scene on the lake. There are breathtaking views of the water and, in the middle distance, the Alps; there are olive groves and flowering trees and flowerbeds in abundance. The principal noise here is wind. An heiress out of Henry James—Ella Walker, whose family owned the Hiram Walker distillery—married a Prince von Thurn und Taxis and purchased this choice property from a Swiss hotelier. At eighty-four, childless, Her Serene Highness, Ella, Principessa della Torre e Tasso, willed the whole to the Rockefeller Foundation; now it provides—so goes the old joke—"the leisure of the theory class" and hosts study groups devoted to world peace, world trade, world health. . . .

A dozen men and women spend a month at the conference center engaged on research and creative projects of their own. Last year, I was one of those fortunate few. There were painters, musicians, sociologists, anthropologists, and doctors; they came from all around the world, and mealtimes entailed a polyglot babble. No telemarketers or television sets disturb one's concentration, and box lunches are provided if one wants to eat alone. A sense of privilege is palpable at the Villa Serbelloni, and the mores of this landscaped hill are those of ancient times. Gardeners tip their cloth caps. Noiseless maids change linens daily and waiters glide through banquet rooms; the grappa and the conversation flow.

There are waitresses and waiters also in the Hotel Bellagio, but the former wear miniskirts and bring drinks to blackjack tables and the latter say, "I'll be your server, how are we doing today?" When you ask for wine or water, the answer is "No problem," and the ambient noise or "surround sound" is loud; an empty room means a space without commerce, and the rooms stay full. If the estate above Lake Como provides a pampered privacy, then the Bellagio Resort Hotel urges the opposite; unlike the silent villa, where isolation is jealously guarded, the palaces of Nevada embrace all those who pay.

The "reality"—that thing in quotes—of Las Vegas is mind-boggling and well known. It has been widely described. This is the fastest-growing city in the U.S.A. Its campy imitations render it original; nowhere else—except perhaps in Disneyworld or at the occasional World's Fair— can the visitor move so rapidly from Italy to Germany or

Japan and the Wild West. Indeed, with the perceived increase in the threat level to Americans abroad, it may well be that this variety of tourism will replace true travel in the future; why put yourself at risk in Cairo or Hong Kong when you can come to Las Vegas with no passport and on the comparative cheap? Only a titillating version of terror attends the roulette wheel or the poker table, and the wages of this sort of sin can be a bonanza in chips. . . .

The town feels immune to recession; prize fighters and singers continue to work, and the microcosmic world expands—or so it would seem—without end. London Bridge and the Eiffel Tower are available as site-sights on this irrigated "strip" of sand; scale versions of the Brooklyn Bridge and the Statue of Liberty represent New York. There are hotels called The Mirage and Mandalay Bay and Treasure Island with its buccaneer motif. A tiger attacked its handler onstage last fall at The Mirage, though the man—Roy Horn of Siegfried & Roy—had been performing with wild animals for forty years. A honeymooning pair who watched weren't sure, they said when interviewed, if the mauling was part of the act.

High-heeled showgirls, off duty, strut past; men puff on Havana cigars. Fabricated butterflies festoon the potted palms. In ten minutes you can travel from the Hotel Venetian—with its gondoliers and blue canals adjacent to the parking lot—to the Bellagio's dancing fountain and its overarching glass canopy designed by Dale Chihuly. There are restaurants and galleries and places to shop in abundance; there's a constant flow of cooling air and constant calibrated light above the slot machines.

The Bellagio Resort Hotel, however, seems to have been born full-blown as "concept," then provided with a name. There's no intrinsic reason for the sobriquet "Bellagio"; the place could just as well be called Firenze or Milano or Positano or Taormina—and even the Italian referent is vague. Perhaps its original owners had a relative from Como; perhaps some design consultant thought the word suggested class. There's a road called Bellagio in tony Bel Air; maybe

that's what they copied instead. I have seen the name Bellagio on restaurants and beachfront condominiums and hand-
bags; it's a free-floating allusion by now. . . .

In any case, Stephen A. Wynn—the resort's presiding genius—has sold his stake and moved along, installing his Pi-
cassos and Cézannes in another gallery; the show in the "museum" when I visited was a selection of Andy Warhol
celebrity portraits. Jacqueline Onassis and Elizabeth Taylor
stared out at the passersby from their glistening silk screens.
The village of Bellagio felt very far away indeed from its
namesake in Nevada, where more people watched the fountains in a single undulation than I saw at the edge of Lake
Como during the whole month of March.

What to make of it, therefore—what's in a name? As Juliet so famously urged the air, "A rose by any other" title
would retain its odor, and if Capulet and Montague were
called Maria and Tony they'd sing much the same refrain. If
"a rose is a rose is a rose," as Gertrude Stein reminds us, then
the habit of naming seems redundant; in every case—by implication in the previous and explication in this present paragraph—we quote and quote and quote.

Two related episodes, though the relation may seem distant:
I am standing by a swimming pool in Sicily. It is February
1970. Mount Etna has been busy; for the two weeks of our
stay in Taormina, smoke clouds have covered its crest. At
night, however, the flame is visible. It rises and falls continually, a red cone across the valley. I face it, trying to sleep.
We have been scouting locations for a film: Palermo, Siracusa, Agricento, Catania—a long string of "Jolly Hotels,"
where the food served is illustrated in laminated photographs
on the elevator walls.

I have been working on a screenplay; my collaborator will
direct the movie that we write. It is based, and not all that
loosely, on my first novel; the money has been raised. Our
troupe flies south from Rome. We joke about "a holding pattern over Catania" as the definition of caution; things have

not been going well. The director has stomach trouble. His remedy appears to be cold white wine and oranges; we have these necessities delivered to the pool. They arrive in quantity. The financiers are caricature moguls; they want our hero to ride a motorcycle through the Mediterranean's turf. They would like a little soft-focused sex in the credits and a lot of it everywhere else.

It is chilly by the pool. Because we are in Sicily, however, and believe it should be warm, we remove our shirts. Our Italian is not good. The poolside phone keeps ringing, and we take turns taking messages. We tell the desk clerk that it's only the *scrittore* and *registra* by the pool; he needn't bother bothering with calls, we need to concentrate. We toss an orange back and forth. The director has some skill at juggling; he juggles four at a time. When the phone distracts him, he drops the oranges; they split. He picks up the receiver and, furious, shouts, "There's nobody here. Do you understand me? Nobody!"

I laugh. I tell him about Polyphemus and *The Odyssey*, as if he does not know. Local legend has it that the Cyclops flung a boulder from this part of the Sicilian shore, after Odysseus blinded and escaped him; we open our third bottle and prepare to try again. He needs a new concept, decides the director, an altogether new approach. He throws a curve; I try a change of pace. He throws a knuckler; I miss. The orange falls into the pool.

A train passes, rumbling, beneath us. We agree that all through Europe the most valuable Riviera frontage belongs to public transport. In America they'd rip up the tracks and rail bed and build condominiums. We watch while the cars disappear. I suggest we opt for silence in the scene; he says these folks are voluble. I want their gestures to be hieratic and their language restrained; we recite the lines with which we've agreed the movie should begin. I feed him a pop fly. His return throw is wild; it also falls into the pool. For no obvious reason, it floats. His stomach feels better, says the director; the wine has done the trick, and he is feeling no pain. We spend ten minutes earnestly at work.

A blood orange sinks. We wonder if that's telltale somehow, and if we can use it: citrus fruit in water, jostling, tumbling in on a deserted beach because a freighter sank. We take a break. The sun appears and Mount Etna ignites—I could swear it. We stand together at the shallow end, an immense sense of achievement hovering between us, a feeling of good fellowship, of two heads as better than one. . . .

They will make the movie. It will be atrocious—too many cooks turning broth into bilge.

We empty the remaining oranges into the pool but do not swim. The telephone rings ceaselessly. We leave the pool. It stops.

Homer called Sicily "Land of the Sun," but the days I spent in Siracusa all were drenched by rain. It was the season for wet weather, and the Archaeological Park had few other visitors; I sat alone on the stone benches of the amphitheater and tried to imagine *Oedipus Tyrannos* or the *Oresteia* playing out beneath me. It did not work. Odysseus, of course, found various excitements there, and once the kingdom had been powerful indeed—a kind of ur-America in its self-confident reach. Having begun as a colony of Greece, it soon outstripped its mother country and, by the fifth century B.C., was a commercial and cultural center of the known world. One ruler, Hiero 1, had been a patron of Aeschylus; another hosted Plato, though Dionysius the Elder—an amateur poet and playwright—seems to have done so by throwing the philosopher (who had arrived at the invitation of his brother-in-law) into jail.

The Roman Consul Marcus Claudius Marcellus, conquering it in 212 B.C., destroyed much of the city. Under imperial rule, the amphitheater was converted from a place for *rhetors* and *rhapsodes* to a colosseum, and blood sports were enacted where late the sweet birds sang. The long history of Sicily thereafter records a long decline; the country is more famous now for its Mafiosi than for, say, *The Leopard*, that great book by Giuseppe Tomasi di Lampedusa. And what I saw of the old capital looked like diminution: a town without charm in the rain. My memories of Siracusa are wine-soaked and self-pitying; Gelon's Temple and the fort and narrow cobbled alleys seemed a momentary stay in the confusion of modernity, a sodden stopping place for tourists and a photo op.

But the original in Sicily is beauty itself when compared to its namesake in upstate New York. That whole central region has suffered of late, its once-flourishing economy a distant memory at best. The countryside and nearby cities all seem in poverty's thrall. Yet Rochester, Auburn, Albany, Buffalo—even Utica and Binghamton—look to have weathered the downturn with greater resilience; Syracuse feels broken-backed, a town of large snowfall accumulations and unemployment and small hope.

I drove to see Raymond Carver there in October 1987. The university where he taught sits on a hill, and the surrounding streets possess some vitality still. Ray's house was book-strewn, filled with light, and we spoke about the last of the short stories in *Cathedral*, his description of and homage to Chekhov's final hours that would prove self-reflexive. It is Carver's own last testament, though it signals what might well have been a new direction for his work. He was clear-eyed when I came, and not pretending that the cancer would remit; he and his wife Tess Gallagher were planning to head west where, in short order, he would die.

It was, in fact, the reason for my visit; we both knew that we would not meet again. My stay was brief; I did not want to weary him, and though he refused to conserve it, his energy was low. We discussed, as always, books, the ones we'd read or planned to read, the ones we hoped it was in us to write, the memory of our shared friend John Gardner. I had visited Ray's house before, at night in winter, and have returned in springtime since—but this memory of Syracuse is autumnal, sere.

The writer and his implements, the journals of the great Russian doctor he was reading, the sandwich he made out of mustard and cheese. . . . When I think of that last morning—

Carver quoting Chekhov in a town that quotes the town in Sicily—I think how all is repetition, recapitulation, variation on a theme. He had been trying to preserve in art what faded from his life.

My wife and I are cleaning out our attic, and we found a box full of maps. Small guides to Paris and Barcelona and London and Rome, large ones of Spain and Italy and Great Britain and France all felt well-worn and pliable; less so were the maps of places visited decades ago only briefly. There were ferry schedules from Woods Hole and Brindisi and Tortola and Oban. There were brochures from Goteborg and Hong Kong and Vienna and Bangkok and Berlin. In the spirit of triage, we unfolded these sheets, and I started to throw them away. The roads of Cape Breton and roads around Athens had penciled-in markers and arrows; I must have followed them once. . . .

Soon enough we were driving down Memory Lane, attempting to remember where we'd been, and when, and why. The Raffles Hotel in Singapore commended itself; so too did the Hotel Residence Duc de Bourgogne in Bruges. We had stayed in them long years before and could not jettison these markers of our shared romantic youth. The Restaurante-Bar Gran Vitel in Bogota announced its history and menu, along with photographs of chefs and rooms now no doubt remodeled or wrecked. A card listed room rates for the "Yasa Samudra" on Kuta Beach in Bali; that hut on the south Java Sea—"Breakfast and Service Charge Included"—once cost us nine dollars a day. There were maps of Uxmal and Chichen Itza and Kyoto and Dublin—a jumble of geographies and places forgotten or dimly recalled. There was advice on "Where to Go in Hamburg" and "This Week in Istanbul" and elaborate instructions on "How to See Nikko." There were fifty illustrated pages on "The Crown Jewels of Iran." Less sumptuous, and produced by the Government Printing Office in December 1970, was a dog-eared, fraying pamphlet on the city of Kabul.

Here is a pair of paragraphs from "Sightseeing in Kabul."

NOON GUN. Originally part of the fortifications of Sher-dawaza Hill, the gun faithfully announces the noon hour each day. The location of the Noon Gun offers a fine view of Kabul University and the Paghman Mountains.

MAUSOLEUM OF KING NADIR SHAH. Situated east of the city on a hill, this marble edifice is an impressive tribute to the man who rescued the country from anarchy in 1929. From the mausoleum there is a fine view of the old city of Kabul, the walls, and the ancient citadel Bala Hissar.

What remains of all of this; how do the schedules of tram lines convey, in the present, the past? A printed watercolor illustration of "The Living Goddess" fairly reeks of Kathmandu. I need only look at an old map of Rhodes to remember the feel of the thick pants I wore, the light on the sea wall, the flavor of sea urchin eggs. Unfolding a brochure on a Martello Tower in St. Johns, I remember the dog in the back seat and how, when I walked him, he lunged after sheep. Proust wrote of these matters at eloquent length, and I don't mean to rehearse the obvious: Kabul is not the place it was, and the memory of places visited is not the same as being there. Things change.

But it seems to me quotation is a constant; it's how we preserve what we keep. If a menu or hotel brochure can evoke in its vivid immediacy a place or time far distant, then what we unfold when we open old charts is memory retrieved. Old letters and journals and maps and photographs each serve the same function as guide. It's a form of dreaming, really, a return to the experience of innocence— and some of those who read these words will think of William Blake. His *Songs of Innocence and Experience* have become, at least in part, a part of common parlance; when someone says, "Tiger, tiger burning bright" or "Little lamb, who made thee," it's not necessarily the case they know they're quoting Blake. When the long-legged models on the fashion runway offer the new "retro" style, it's a mode most are too young to recognize from previous fashion and use. But it's quotation nevertheless, a tip of the cap to designs of the past that, next year, will be last year's look. . . .

Edgar Degas received permission to make copies at the Louvre in 1853, when he was eighteen. He copied Ingres and Poussin, among others, and traces of their influence would linger in his brush stroke and palette till old age. Later he had this to say: "The Masters must be copied over and over again, and it is only after proving yourself a good copyist that you should reasonably be permitted to draw a radish from nature." The "radish from nature" is a box full of maps; the country or city they point to is referenced by memory (you have heard that song before; there was a full moon, that "Old Devil Moon"; you were standing on a blanket on the lawn at Tanglewood), and the reality of such a text or image is a quotation retrieved.

If a writer has been writing long enough, this kind of verbal retrieval must surely come to pass. Repetition is as natural as breath. When a singer known for a particular tune goes out on tour, it would disappoint the audience if the old standard were not at some point in the concert performed; if a comedian has a familiar routine, the old chestnut must be duly roasted. Our themes declare themselves at least in part because recurrent; the texts of one's twenties and thirties will predict what follows on. Early Hemingway and Faulkner give a template for the late. The characteristic syntax of, say, Elizabeth Bowen was established at a certain stage and would have been as hard to alter as her handwriting; the semicolon in this sentence is a form of signature, and the ellipsis with which it ends is habitual in Ford Madox Ford. . . . Imagine for an instant that a trapeze artist shifted beats and tried to improvise a meeting with an airborne partner; such a performance *requires* rehearsal, quotation: split-second timing not subject to change. We leave, in short, our fingerprints all over every page, and if I've written that before, why, then I've written that before. . . .

There's a part of the cerebral cortex where such referents are stored. I knew a woman who suffered a series of strokes—catastrophic and finally mortal. She could not remember proper names or what she had eaten for breakfast, or if. She was unable to read. Astonishingly, however, she retained her memory for tunes and poems learned when young; she could recite great swatches of Longfellow and songs in Welsh, and, bedridden for years, she would entertain herself and those who sat beside her by repeating entire narratives from the *Mabinogion* or "The Day Is Done" or "My Lost Youth" or "The Birds of Killingworth." It was as though the lines were inscribed on the ceiling she stared at— verse after verse, rhyme after rhyme—and they kept her company throughout her long travail.

Sometimes quotation is conscious: a politician with a slogan, an actress reciting a speech. The "inspirational speaker" repeats his or her mantra verbatim, with a memorized message "on point." We pepper our discourse with other folks' talk, and if William Shakespeare and Montaigne had copyrighted what they wrote, their estates would be quadruple actual size. That "there is no new thing under the sun"—itself a quote from Ecclesiastes—is of course not news. It's why we know what to expect from a line and when a line is apt. Boilerplate invades the boardroom, the classroom, the living room; how often in a single day do we produce or phrase a single new idea?

When I hear in my own voice—as I do now increasingly—my father's intonation, it's a tone that feels foreordained; no matter how closely I monitor myself, I can't keep from repetition or the twice-told tale. Old jokes, old stories, old friends or enemies in their fixed patterns of behavior—so that we recognize and smile or recognize and scowl—all are commonplace. Indeed, they're necessary, functional; we don't create the alphabet each time we write a sentence or invent the steering wheel every time we drive. If something has been said before, and well, why alter it for variety's sake? "What oft was thought, but ne'er so well expressed" (Alexander Pope, *Essay on Criticism*, Part II, line 97) can just as well remain verbatim on the page.

This is not so much a function of memory or education as of our system of discourse; it's impossible *not* to repeat. One word leads to another as the night the day. It's how rote learning operates, and associative memory: the pleasures of a nursery rhyme of which children know the chorus and shout it delightedly out. The actor, singer, or politician is in this sense a particular instance of the more general case. Conversation has quotation at its epicenter; it's the engine that drives dialogue, both molecule and bond. *All* talk, it seems to me, is formulaic in structure; we repeat an anecdote or a routine. At other times we counterfeit spontaneity, pretending what we say is spur-of-the-moment and new. Quotation is the building block of language, its very marrow and pith.

Had I written "pith and marrow," those who recognize the phrase would see it as a formula; as a chiasmus (where the terms of a phrase are inverted) it's a small-scale variation on a small-scale theme. We say "quote unquote" but don't really mean it; what we mean at the end of a line is "end quote" and not a retraction of what went before. We remember where we've been. We repeat what we have learned. The third and fourth of this paragraph's first five sentences are structured similarly; they begin with the first person plural pronoun and each have seven syllables; their second word—a verb—begins with the letters "re." There all resemblance ends. Yet the retentive eye, attentive ear will find the lines echoic; this kind of repetitive structure is not the exception but rule. . . .

In the month my wife and I resided in Bellagio, fighting began in Iraq; the dogs of war had slipped their leash, though the baying seemed far off. It was hard not to refer to the great parable by Thomas Mann, and how the "magic mountain's"

denizens were inconvenienced by what became World War
I. Herr Settembrini on *his* mountaintop would recognize the
grounds; it isn't easy to gain access to the Villa Serbelloni,
and the gates that give out on the village are locked.

Our insularity was less than total, however; such headlines
vault water and walls. Newspapers can be bought. There was
no one at the conference center who had anything to say about
America that was anything other than appalled; the Russians
and the Egyptians and the Tamils and the Tuvas, though they
tried to be polite about it, believed we were governed by mad-
ness—a nightmare of empire. The air attack of 1991 and "Operation Shock and Awe" of 2003 felt eerily dissimilar, though
cut from the same bolt of cloth. The pairing here—Bush,
Bush, Iraq, Iraq—seemed not a quotation but rant. It was as
though we'd heard and read and discussed the war a decade
previous, but it was no longer amusing; the jokes about
"Shrub" and "Bush league" turned acid on the tongue.

So we walked beneath the ancient fort, its picturesque
rubble and jumble of rock. Attempting to take comfort in the
long reach of history, we spoke of others in anxiety who had
walked this way before. During the Middle Ages, Bellagio
had been involved in the conflicts between the communes of
Milan and Como, and between the Guelph and the Ghi-
belline factions the fortress on the promontory changed
hands three times by siege. In 1369 the Viscontis, one of Milan's ruling families, decided that it was more an inconven-
ience than an asset (it had become a lair for German mercenaries), and had the buildings razed.

There has been fighting since. The mountain passes and
the hills have only rarely known peace. This area was occupied by Germans during World War II; they leveled olive
groves to make way for landing strips and cut down cypress
trees in order to improve their lines of sight. Mussolini, attempting to escape to Switzerland, was captured just across
the lake; it is rumored he dressed as a woman and his car-
riage was chock-full of gold. The Italians dragged him back
south to Milano, where his bullet-riddled body was hung
out on display.

Pliny the Younger wrote of his villas—he owned two—in what was then called Comum: "One is set high on a cliff . . . and overlooks the lake. Supported by rock, as if by the stilt-like shoes of the actors in tragedy. I call it Tragedia. It enjoys a broad view of the lake, which the ridge on which it stands divides in half. . . . From its spacious terrace, the descent to the lake is gentle."[1]

I quote him in translation and nearly two thousand years later. Tragic actors no longer wear stilts, but the support of the rock face has not worn away, and the Villa Serbelloni still offers a "broad view." White ferries ply the blue water, and for the month of March the lake stayed calm. There were olive trees and cypresses waiting to be planted; there was a backhoe by the harbor, men working forklifts, and piles of manure. The camellias bloomed and faded; then the mimosas began.

The library where once the dying Ella Walker lay— reclusive in old age, attended only by her servants—has volumes donated by those who have passed through. Another of the Thurn und Taxis properties—Duino Castle, near Trieste—sheltered the poet Rilke; he composed his *Duino Elegies* while waiting for words from the wind. I read them, tried to hear them—*Wer, wenn Ich schrie*—and tried to write lines of my own. It did not work. Each day before dawn I would sit at my desk and attempt the final chapter of the novel I was working on; each afternoon I would read what I'd written and tinker and correct the pages and then tear them up.

The executive director of the Fondazione Rockefeller is the widow of its previous director. The presiding spirit of the villa, Madame Gianna Celli is efficient and accomplished and rail-thin. Her staff and hired workmen and even her visitors quail. She has seen it all, she says without saying; she has known your elders and your betters and is by your antics unimpressed. The coat is adequate, but the shoes require shining and the shirt is a disgrace. The Nobel laureate before you did a better job with accents, the cabinet minister here just last week was wearing the same trousers, except they had been pressed. . . .

La Senora Celli has this to say at breakfast: "You are insane, you will die in the sand. You Americans don't understand how everyone will hate you now, how serious things are." Gianna eats great quantities of fruit and, since the outbreak of mad cow disease, will not permit the Serbelloni's cooks to buy or use red meat. She is imperious, opinionated, fierce. "The gardeners," she says, "insist on planting by the moon. And they are always wrong. These people get everything wrong. The Umbrians are sorrowful, the Tuscans arrogant, the people of Lombardy sad. In Como, for example, you might perhaps see somebody smiling, but you will never hear the sound of laughter in the streets. These people cannot cook," she says. "Their idea of high cuisine is rice with three slices of fish." When I ask her if there's anyone she in fact admires, Gianna pauses, shakes her head. And then her face brightens—she does have an answer: "The dead."

Notes

In Praise of Imitation

1. *Webster's New Collegiate Dictionary* (Springfield, MA: G. & C. Merriam, 1951), 414.

2. Charles Caleb Colton, *Lacon: or, Many things in few words, addressed to those who think*, vol. 1 (New York: E. Bliss and E. White, 1822–23), 123.

3. Nicholas Delbanco, *The Lost Suitcase: Reflections on the Literary Life* (New York: Columbia University Press, 2000), 27–28.

4. John Barth, *The Friday Book: Essays & Other Nonfiction* (New York: G. P. Putnam's Sons, 1984), 84–85.

5. A. K. Ramanujan, *Uncollected Poems and Prose* (New York: Oxford University Press, 2000), 68.

6. Cyril Connolly, *Enemies of Promise* (New York: Persea Books, 1983), 109.

7. Ibid. 119.

The Dead

1. William Shakespeare, *The Riverside Shakespeare* (Boston: Houghton Mifflin, 1974), 880 (*I Henry IV* 5.4.77–83).

2. Ibid. 1185 (*Hamlet, Prince of Denmark* 5.2.358).

3. Dudley Fitts, *Poems from the Greek Anthology in English Paraphrase* (New York: New Directions, 1956), 108, 113.

4. Thomas Nashe, "In Time of Pestilence," *The Oxford Book of English Verse*, ed . Arthur Quiller-Couch (New York: Oxford University Press, 1957), 208.

5. E. M. Forster, *Aspects of the Novel* (New York: Harcourt, Brace & World, 1955), 48.

6. William Butler Yeats, *The Collected Poems of W. B. Yeats* (New York: Macmillan, 1961), 344.

7. C. P. Cavafy, *Collected Poems*, ed. George Savides, tr. E. Keeley and P. Sherrard (Princeton: Princeton University Press, 1992), 52.

An Old Man Mad About Writing

1. Cited in Alan Judd, *Ford Madox Ford* (Cambridge: Harvard University Press, 1991), 438.

2. Ford Madox Ford, *The March of Literature* (New York: Dial Press, 1938), vi.

3. Ibid. 10.

4. Judd, *Ford Madox Ford*, 428–429.

5. Arthur Mizener, *The Saddest Story: A Biography of Ford Madox Ford* (New York: World Publishing Company, 1971), 447.

6. Ford, *The March of Literature*, vi.

7. Ibid. 740–741.

8. Ibid. 355–356.

9. Ibid. 219.

10. Ibid. 5.

11. Judd, *Ford Madox Ford*, 432, quoting Macauley, "The Dean In Exile," *Shenandoah* IV (Spring 1953).

12. Ford, *The March of Literature*, 698–699.

13. Ibid. 849–850.

14. Ibid. 840.

15. Ibid. 843.

16. Ibid. 486–487.

17. Ibid. 4.

18. Ibid. 850.

19. Joseph Brewer, "Ford Madox Ford: a Memoir," *The Saturday Review of Literature*, 7/8/39.

20. Ford, *The March of Literature*, 845.

21. Ford Madox Ford, *No More Parades*, in *Parade's End* (New York: Alfred A. Knopf, 1950), 362.

22. Ibid. 454.

Anywhere Out of the World

1. Marco Polo, *The Adventures of Marco Polo*, ed. R. E. Latham (New York: Penguin, 1982), 3.

2. John Julius Norwich, ed., *A Taste for Travel* (New York: Knopf, 1985), 6–7.

3. Ibid. 1.

4. Laurence Kelly, ed., *St. Petersburg, a Travellers' Companion* (New York: Atheneum, 1981), 269–270 (ms. in the Sloane Papers in the British Museum).

Letter from Namibia

1. *Saturday Star* ("SA's Biggest selling Saturday Newspaper"), August 10, 2002, 1.

2. This information is culled from Gerald Cubitt and Peter Joyce, *This Is Namibia* (London: New Holland Publishers, 1992), 7–26.

3. Henno Martin, *The Sheltering Desert* (Jeppstown: A. D. Donker Publishers, 1983), 9.

4. Ibid. 323.

5. Much of this information derives from Stephen T. Bassett, *Rock Paintings of South Africa* (Capetown: David Philip, 2001).

6. Jon Manchip White, *The Land God Made in Anger* (London: George Allen & Unwin, 1969), 233–234.

Northern Lights

1. Hermann Palsson, introduction to *Hrafnkel's Saga and Other Stories* (London: Penguin Classics, 1971), 8.

2. Michael Crichton, *Eaters of the Dead* (New York: Knopf, 1976). Page numbers hereinafter cited are drawn from this text.

3. E. L. Bredsdorff, *The Penguin Companion to European Literature* (Hardmondsworth: Penguin, 1969), 118.

4. Isak Dinesen, "The Deluge at Norderney," *Seven Gothic Tales* (New York: Modern Library, 1934), 25.

5. Isak Dinesen, "The Roads Around Pisa," *Seven Gothic Tales* (New York: Modern Library, 1934), 165.

6. Isak Dinesen, "The Supper at Elsinore," *Seven Gothic Tales* (New York: Modern Library, 1934). 253.

7. Ibid. 221.

8. Isak Dinesen, "Sorrow-Acre," *Winter's Tales* (New York: Random House, 1942), 29.

9. Ibid. 30–31.

10. Ibid. 41.

11. Ibid. 66–67.

12. Vladimir Nabokov, *Pale Fire* (New York: Everyman's Library, 1992), 67.

13. Vladimir Nabokov, *Lectures on Russian Literature* (New York: Harvest/HBJ, 1981), 320.

14. Nabokov, *Pale Fire*, 171.

15. Nabokov, *Pale Fire*, 158.

16. Nabokov, *Pale Fire*, 165.

17. Nabokov, *Pale Fire*, 50.

18. Nabokov, *Pale Fire*, 27.

19. Nabokov, *Pale Fire*, 90.

20. Nabokov, *Pale Fire*, 21.

21. Nabokov, *Pale Fire*, 21.

22. Nabokov, *Pale Fire*, 229.

23. Nabokov, *Pale Fire*, 239.

24. Nabokov, *Pale Fire*, 107.

On Daniel Martin

1. From John Gardner, review of *Daniel Martin*, *Saturday Review*, October 1, 1977. S. O'Nan, ed., *On Writers and Writing* (New York: Addison-Wesley, 1994), 134–139.

2. John Fowles, *Daniel Martin* (London: Jonathan Cape, 1977), 7.

3. Ibid. 704.

4. Ibid.

5. Ibid. 9.

6. Ibid. 8.

7. Ibid. 11.

8. Ibid. 14.

9. Ibid. 16.

10. Ibid.

11. Ibid. 8.

12. Ibid. 17.

13. Ibid. 24.

14. John Fowles, *Poems* (New York: Ecco Press, 1973), 67–68.

15. Fowles, *Daniel Martin*, 197.

16. Ibid. 207.

17. Ibid. 224.

18. Ibid. 246.

19. Ibid. 264.

20. Ibid. 164.

21. Ibid. 302.

22. Ibid. 371.

23. Ibid. 249–254.

24. Ibid. 16.

Strange Type

1. Malcolm Lowry, *Selected Poems of Malcolm Lowry*, ed. Earle Birney (San Francisco: City Lights, 1962), 79.

2. Ibid. 78.

3. Ibid. 75.

4. Ernest Hemingway, *A Farewell to Arms* (New York: Charles Scribner's Sons, 2003), 185.

5. Malcolm Lowry, *The Selected Letters of Malcolm Lowry*, ed. M. B. Lowry (New York: J. B. Lippincott, 1965), 3 (Letter to Conrad Aiken).

6. Christopher Marlowe, *The Tragical History of Dr. Faustus* (New York: Appleton-Century-Crofts, 1950), 59–60 (scene 14).

7. Malcolm Lowry, *Under the Volcano* (New York: J. B. Lippincott, 1965), 34.

8. Lowry, *Selected Letters*, 39 (Letter to Harold Matson).

In Defense of Quotation

1. G. Facchetti and C. O. Pagnoni, *"Renovation Project"*: *The Bellagio Study and Conference Center* (Rome: Giquattordici Progettazione), 7.